Vegetarian Food For Carnivores

Vegetarian Food For Carnivores

Sarah McLean

YouCaxton Publications
Oxford & Shrewsbury

ISBN 978-1-912419-84-5

Printed and bound in Great Britain.
Published by YouCaxton Publications 2020
YCBN: 01

YouCaxton Publications
enquiries@youcaxton.co.uk

For Kate, who has always understood and supported my dreams.

CONTENTS

Nutritious

Delicious

Good for the Planet

Good for you

Author's Note

I trained as a chef when I left school and worked in the catering trade for a couple of years. As a chef, I struggled with the ethics of using meat and eventually left to train as a nurse. However, my interest and love of cooking remained, but became tailored over time with 20 years of Nursing knowledge. During my Nursing career, I have seen from first hand experience that diet and health go hand in hand, the way you eat can effect your long term health, quality of life and actual life expectancy. The way you eat today is the most important investment you can make for your future.

The idea for this cookery book was conceived due to an impending visit from our Australian Uncle Jimmy, a confirmed meat eater with many years experience of barbecues and the meat orientated Australian diet.

I looked at traditional meat dishes and set about converting them to recipes that could be made with Quorn or other meat free alternatives.

After weeks of planning, Uncle Jimmy came to stay and wolfed down every one of my meals for 3 weeks [even having seconds !], raving about my cooking. I thought he had remembered we were vegetarian, so never mentioned it, but was extremely relieved that he had enjoyed my food so much.

It wasn't until he was picked up from our house by vegetarian /vegan cousins, got into their car and said with a heavy heart, 'I suppose I will have to eat vegetarian food now', that we realised the meat free dishes had been so tasty and similar to their meat counterparts that he hadn't given the vegetarian question a second thought.

This gave me the idea for this book. Not just another vegetarian cookery book, but a book that provides a feasible alternative to meat recipes, without losing any of the taste.

It is a recipe book that can be used by anyone, from a meat eating family who are expecting vegetarians to stay, to the vegetarian family expecting an 'Uncle Jimmy' to stay, to the grandparents struggling to cook for their vegetarian/ vegan grandson/ daughter.

It can simply be used to help people reduce their meat intake.

Thanks to Uncle Jimmy, I hope I have created a book that has long been needed on the market.

These recipes can be used for people who need to reduce their fat and cholesterol intake as, Quorn and other meat free alternatives on the market are very low in fat and cholesterol, while still being an excellent source of protein. I have deliberately reduced the saturated fat content by using olive oil in most of the recipes rather than butter, so the majority of fats used are 'good' fats that are beneficial to health. I have occasionally sneaked in some butter as I felt the taste justified it, but this can be replaced with olive oil if wished.

Meat replacement products often take less time to prepare as they are bought in pre-prepared packets that simply need tipping into the pan in order to cook. As meat is taken out of the equation, the risk of food poisoning is drastically reduced.

For those people who want or need to reduce their salt intake, low salt alternatives are available for Marmite, vegetable stock cubes and gravy powder.

It is important to wash fruit, salad and vegetables before cooking in order to remove any pesticides and to prevent food poisoning. I take the extra precaution of peeling, then washing potatoes and root vegetables. I have not stipulated 'peeling and washing vegetables' in every recipe, due to space. Also, some people choose not to peel all their vegetables, but hopefully, will know how important it is to wash them thoroughly before food preparation. '

Sarah McLean, June 2019

Food For Thought!

Why Do We Need To Eat Less Meat?

The question, 'What shall we have to eat today?' has far reaching consequences.

The answer to this will determine the type of future our children will have, and perhaps the destiny of our species and many of the animals, microbes and plants inhabiting planet Earth.

By reducing our meat intake we can; Become healthier humans;

1. Meat is potentially cancer causing.
    A recent report by the World Health Organisation categorised processed meats as level 1 carcinogens, placing them in the same category as cigarettes and alcohol. The organisation categorised red meat as a level 2a- probable carcinogen.
2. Cardiovascular health.
    Data has shown time and time again that red meat is linked with high cholesterol, and in turn, increases the risk for cardiovascular disease such as heart attacks and strokes.
3. Eating meat increases your risk of type 2 diabetes.
    According to a report published by JAMA Internal Medicine, eating red or processed meat can, over time, increase the risk of developing type 2 diabetes.
4. You have a better chance of staying slim.
    Research has shown that eating red meat has been linked to obesity. A survey by Quorn suggests that if every UK household switched beef mince to Quorn just once a week, the nation would save 370 billion calories a year.
5. Meat could put your brain at risk.
    Meat contains iron which, when eaten in excess can raise the levels of iron in the brain and may increase the risk of developing Alzheimer's Disease, according to a study from UCLA. When iron accumulates in the brain, myelin- a fatty tissue that coats nerve fibres is destroyed. This disrupts brain communication, and signs of Alzheimer's appear.
6. Meat contains added hormones.
    To make animals grow at an accelerated rate, the industry feeds or injects them with artificial hormones. In a study published in the Archives of Internal Medicine, researchers believe the hormones or hormone type compounds in red meat increase the risk of breast cancer by attaching to specific hormone receptors on the tumours.
7. The Livestock Industry contributes to the growth of antibiotic-resistant diseases.
    Animals are farmed in closer proximity and are therefore at greater risk of disease.

The response from the farms is to feed their animals with large quantities of antibiotics. As bacteria is constantly evolving, this can lead to antibiotic resistant strains known through the media as 'Superbugs'.

8. You will reduce the risk of Food Poisoning.

   The U.S Department of Agriculture (USDA) reports that 70% of food poisoning is caused by contaminated animal flesh.

9. You will live longer without meat.

   According to a study of over 70,000 published in the Journal JAMA Internal Medicine, vegetarians were 12 per cent less likely to have died during a 6 year follow up than their meat- eating peers.

   Vegetarian men live to an average of 83.3 years compared with non-vegetarian men, who live to an average of 73.8 years. Vegetarian women live to an average of 85.7 years which is 6.1 years longer than non-vegetarian women according to the Adventist Health Study.

   As an added bonus, a few years ago, some life insurance firms even offered vegetarians cheaper premiums on the basis they were healthier and lived longer.

10. Animal cruelty.

    It is sometimes easy to forget that the steak on your plate was part of a living creature. Millions of animals are killed each year, with a huge number of these being produced in factory farms. Switching to a less meat, or a no meat diet is voting to end the cruel treatment of animals.

11. Help to fight climate change.

    Meat production is a huge contributor to greenhouse gas emissions, and if we are trying to limit the planetary temperature rise to 1.5°C, we have to address the meat industry.

12. Help save the Amazon from destruction.

    Roughly a quarter of the Earth's land is used for animal grazing. This is a major driver of deforestation and the removal of natural savannah, grasslands and native forests that can never be replaced in their original form.

13. Help to protect endangered species.

    With pastured animals and the vast crops required to feed their confined counterparts taking up so much space, the local wild species are pushed out of the way. Many large herbivores are threatened by 'competition for grazing space, water, a greater risk of disease transmission, and hybridization.' Since 1070, the Earth has lost half its wildlife but tripled its livestock production.

14. Help to protect water sources.

    Water is one of the world's most precious resources and yet it is squandered when it comes to meat production. The use of water for meat production together with the fertilisers used to grow crops, have resulted in more than 600 dead zones in the oceans, along with widespread overgrowth of algae in coastal and freshwater regions which can deplete the oxygen content of the water body.

15. You will save money.

    Vegetarian and vegan meals usually work out less expensive than meat based meals. The Cleveland Clinic found that replacing one omnivore meal with a vegetarian one can save approximately 80 pence per person. This could amount to the equivalent of £2,248 based on a family of 4 reducing their meat intake by 2 meals a day for a year.

Reducing or eliminating meat from your diet has so many benefits. Look better, feel better and save the planet.

Start taking steps today. Improve your health and the planet, one meatless meal at a time.

Instead of contributing to the destruction of your body, the environment, and animal's lives, you'll be on the side of health, sustainability and respect for all living beings.

Your answer to the question of 'What shall we eat today?' can effect a change in all of this, and consequently, may be one of the most important questions we will ever ask.

PASTRY, PIES AND QUICHES

Cornish Pasties

Cheese and Quorn Ham Quiche

No Chicken and Mushroom Pie with Potato Topping

No Chicken and Mushroom Pie in Pastry

County Chicken Free Pie

Roasted Vegetable Pie

Welsh Oggie

Cornish Pasties

These are a popular and versatile alternative to the traditional recipe made with meat.

The traditional form of the Cornish pasty was a complete meal, wrapped in pastry to sustain the working man throughout the day. The pastry kept the meal together and enabled it to be eaten as easily and cleanly as possible, even down the tin mines.

The same principle applies today, and this recipe is excellent for picnics or for a packed lunch.

This recipe makes 6-8 pasties depending on size.

SHORTCRUST PASTRY

10oz (284g) plain flour
½ teaspoon salt
5oz (142g) butter or margarine
approximately 4-5 tablespoons of cold water

FILLING

½ bag (150g) Quorn mince
1 tablespoon olive oil
1 small onion, approximately 4oz (113g), finely chopped
4oz (113g) carrot, peeled and grated
6oz (170g) finely diced potato
4 fluid oz (114mls) stock made with 2 vegetable stock cubes and 1 teaspoon Marmite
1 level teaspoon dried mixed herbs
ground sea salt and freshly ground black pepper
milk to glaze

SHORTCRUST PASTRY METHOD

1. Make the pastry by sieving the flour and salt into a bowl.
2. Rub in the butter or margarine until the mix resembles fine breadcrumbs.
3. Make a well in the centre and gradually add the water, mixing all the time with a knife until the mixture forms a soft dough.
4. Cover and store in the fridge while the filling for the pasties is made.

FILLING METHOD

5. Fry the chopped onion in the olive oil until softened. Add the diced potato and carrot. Continue to cook for a few minutes, stirring well until both are partially cooked.
6. Add the Quorn mince, 4 fluid oz (114mls) stock, mixed herbs, salt and pepper.
7. Gently simmer for about 5-10 minutes, stirring all the time, then set to one side.
8. Roll out the pastry and use a saucer to cut out about 6 circles. Re roll the pastry as necessary. These circles can be made smaller or larger depending on how big the pasties need to be. Obviously, bigger pasties will result in less pasties being made.

9. Place about a tablespoon of the mixture in the centre of each pastry circle.

10. Moisten the edges of the pastry circle with water.

11. Fold in half and seal, flute the edges and brush with milk. The pasties can be shaped so the join is on the top or along the side.

12. Place on a baking tray. Bake in a pre-heated oven 200°C (400°F) or Gas mark 6 for 15 minutes.

13. Reduce the heat to 160°C (325°F) or Gas mark 3, and bake for a further 20 minutes until golden brown. Leave to cool on a wire rack.

Serve hot or cold with a range of salads or simply with cooked vegetables, potatoes and gravy.

Cheese and Quorn Ham Quiche

This is my version of perhaps the best known quiche on the market. I actually think it tastes better than the original. But try it for yourself and see.

This makes 6-8 slices of quiche depending on size.

SHORTCRUST PASTRY

10oz (284g) plain flour
½ teaspoon salt
5oz (142g) butter or hard margarine
5 tablespoons cold water (approximately)

FILLING

12oz (340g) grated, mature cheddar cheese
3oz (85g) Quorn ham slices, finely chopped
3 eggs
¼ pint (140mls) milk
sea salt and freshly ground black pepper

PASTRY METHOD

1. Sieve the flour and salt into a bowl.
2. Rub the butter into the flour until the mixture resembles fine breadcrumbs.
3. Make a well in the centre and add the water gradually, while stirring with a knife, until the pastry forms into a fairly stiff paste.
4. Using a rolling pin, roll the pastry into a circle large enough to line a 10 inch (25½cm) diameter flan dish. Press firmly into the base and sides.
5. Cover with grease proof paper and use dried beans or similar to weigh down.
6. Cook at 190°C (375°F) or Gas mark 5 for 15 minutes. Take out of the oven. Remove the greaseproof paper and cooking beans and add the filling.

FILLING METHOD

7. Grate the cheese and mix in the 3oz (85g) Quorn ham, finely chopped.
8. Beat the eggs in with the milk, mix in the cheese and Quorn Ham, then season well with salt and pepper.
9. Pour into the pastry case and bake in a preheated oven at 180°C (350°F) or Gas mark 4 for a further 30 minutes until the quiche is set in the centre and has turned golden brown.

Serve with a fresh green salad and freshly made bread, or use as part of a buffet or cold table.

No Chicken and Mushroom Pie with Potato Topping

This is a delicious alternative to the usual meat with potato topping type recipe. It is simple to make, and can easily be made the day before. The mushroom ketchup which can be found in most large supermarkets and some delicatessens, really enhances the mushroom flavour.

This recipe makes approximately 4-6 servings depending on size.

INGREDIENTS

300g bag Quorn pieces
1 large onion, peeled and chopped
6oz (170g) mushrooms, wiped with damp kitchen towel and roughly chopped
2 tablespoons olive oil
½ teaspoon mustard powder
1 teaspoon (small) dried mixed herbs
1 tablespoon mushroom ketchup
½ pint (284mls) vegetable stock made with 1 vegetable stock cube

1 dessert spoon gravy powder
ground sea salt and freshly ground black pepper

FOR THE TOPPING

1¾ lb (794g) potatoes, peeled and cut into pieces
½ teaspoon salt
1oz (28g) butter
4oz (113g) strong cheddar cheese, grated
pinch mustard powder
a little milk to mix

METHOD

1. Cook the potatoes in boiling salted water for about 25 minutes until soft. Prepare the filling while the potatoes are cooking.

2. In a large frying pan, fry the onion in the olive oil until softened. Add the mushrooms to the onions, stirring regularly.

3. Mix in the Quorn pieces and cook until well defrosted.

4. Add the mustard powder, mixed herbs, mushroom ketchup, vegetable stock and mix well. Simmer over a low heat for 5-10 minutes. Season well with salt and pepper.

5. Blend the gravy powder with a little water until it resembles a smooth paste and stir into the Quorn mixture. Add a splash more hot water if the mixture appears too thick.

6. Drain the potatoes well, then mash together with the butter, grated cheese and mustard. Add salt and pepper and enough milk to give a smooth consistency.

7. Spread the Quorn mixture on the bottom of a 2 pint oven proof casserole dish and cover with the potato. Decorate the top by making patterns with a fork.

8. Cook in an oven preheated to 180°C (350°F) or Gas mark 4 for 30 - 40 minutes until golden brown on top.

Serve with fresh seasonal vegetables and lashings of gravy.

No Chicken and Mushroom Pie in Pastry

This is one of those recipes that you can use time and time again. I fell upon it by accident when using ingredients at the back of the cupboard when I hadn't had chance to go shopping. I have cooked this for people who still rave about it every time I see them.

This recipe makes approximately 4 - 6 portions depending on size.

INGREDIENTS

1 bag (300g) Quorn pieces
1 small onion, finely chopped
1 clove garlic, crushed
9oz (255g) mushrooms, wiped with damp kitchen towel and chopped
1 tablespoon olive oil
1 tin (295g) condensed mushroom soup
1 vegetable stock cube

ground sea salt and freshly ground black pepper

SHORTCRUST PASTRY

12oz (340g) plain flour, sieved
½ teaspoon salt
6oz (170g) butter or hard margarine
approximately 6 tablespoons cold water
milk or beaten egg to glaze

METHOD

1. In a large frying pan, fry the onions and garlic until softened. Add the mushrooms and continue to cook for a further 5 minutes.

2. Add the Quorn pieces and cook until defrosted.

3. Add the soup, stock cube and season well with salt and pepper. Simmer gently for 5-10 minutes to combine the flavours, then set aside off the heat.

METHOD FOR SHORTCRUST PASTRY

4. Add the salt to the flour and rub in the butter until it resembles fine breadcrumbs.

5. Add the water and stir with a knife until the pastry forms into a dough.

6. Use a deep 9inch (23cm) diameter pie dish. Roll out two thirds of the pastry to a circle larger in size than the pie dish, and line it with the pastry. Pour in the mixture and spread evenly over the base of the dish.

7. Roll out the remaining pastry to cover the top. Moisten the joining edges of the pie with water to seal, lift the pastry top by draping over the rolling pin and place on top of the pie. Trim off the excess pastry round the edges. Pinch the outer edges together to create the pastry crust.

8. Cut a small slit in the centre of the pie to let the steam escape while cooking. Decorate with small leaves cut out of left over pastry, moisten with water before attaching. Brush with milk or beaten egg to glaze the pastry.

9. Cook in the centre of oven at 190°C (375°F) or Gas mark 5 for approximately 30 minutes until the pastry is golden brown.

Serve with potatoes and plenty of fresh, seasonal vegetables.

County Chicken Free Pie

This is a really tasty dish that can be made the day before, refrigerated, and cooked when needed. It is one of those timeless meals that will be enjoyed by adults and children alike.

Serves 4-6 depending on portion size.

INGREDIENTS

1 bag (300g) Quorn pieces
2 medium sized leeks
2oz (56g) butter
1 stock cube
sea salt and freshly ground black pepper
2lb (908g) potatoes, peeled, washed and quatered

1oz (28g) butter
3 tablespoons of milk

CHEESE SAUCE

1oz (28g) butter
1½ oz (42g) plain flour
¾ pint (424mls) milk
6oz (170g) grated, strong cheddar cheese

METHOD

1. Cook the potatoes in boiling salted water until soft, then mash with 1oz (28g) butter and 3 tablespoons of milk

2. While the potatoes are cooking, wash the leeks well and cut into slices. Melt 2oz (56g) butter in a non-stick saucepan and gently cook the leeks over a low heat for about 10 minutes until they are soft, stirring regularly.

3. Add the Quorn pieces and stock cube. Mix well into the leek mixture and continue to cook over a low heat, for a further 5-10 minutes until the Quorn pieces have defrosted and begin to cook in with the other ingredients. Season well with salt and pepper.

METHOD FOR CHEESE SAUCE

4. Make the sauce by melting 1oz (28g) butter in a non-stick pan. Add the flour stirring well to prevent lumps forming, then gradually stir in the milk. I find it much easier to warm the milk first as it speeds up the thickening process and stops the milk from catching on the bottom of the pan.

5. If the sauce gets lumpy at any stage, simply whisk with a balloon whisk and this will get rid of the lumps. Continue to stir well until the sauce thickens. Turn down the heat to prevent the sauce from sticking. Season well with salt and pepper

6. Stir 4oz (113g) grated cheese into the sauce over a low heat until the cheese melts.

7. Pour the Cheese sauce over the leek and Quorn mixture and stir well to incorporate the ingredients.

8. Transfer this mixture to the bottom of a casserole dish and top with the mashed potato. Sprinkle remaining grated cheese over the top and cook in a preheated oven 180°C (350°F) or Gas mark 4 for 30-40 minutes until golden brown.

Serve with seasonal vegetables.

Roasted Vegetable Pie

This is a fantastic, cold winter day favourite. The cooking smells seem to pervade through the house and the rich flavour of this pie is well worth trudging through the snow for.

This dish serves 4 - 6 depending on portion size.

FILLING

Approximately 3-4 tablespoons of olive oil
½ courgette, sliced
1 medium carrot, chopped
1 medium parsnip, chopped
5 shallots, sliced
6 chestnut mushrooms, wiped with damp kitchen towel and chopped
1 stick of celery, chopped
1 clove garlic, crushed
1 bag (300g) Quorn pieces
1 tablespoon tomato puree

1 teaspoon Marmite and 1 stock cube dissolved in ¼ pint (140mls) hot water
½ teaspoon dried rosemary
1 tablespoon balsamic vinegar
1 dessert spoon gravy powder
ground sea salt and freshly ground black pepper

SHORTCRUST PASTRY

12oz (340g) plain flour, sieved
½ teaspoon salt
6oz (170g) butter or hard margarine
approximately 6 tablespoons cold water
milk or beaten egg to glaze

METHOD FOR PIE FILLING

1. In an oven proof casserole dish, roast the pre-prepared courgette, carrot, parsnip and shallots in the olive oil in a preheated oven 220°C (425°F) or Gas mark 7 for 15- 20 minutes. Turn over with a fish slice and add the mushrooms and garlic. Return to the oven for about another 10 minutes until the vegetables are well roasted.

2. Reduce the heat to 180°C (370°F) or Gas mark 4. Add the Quorn pieces, tomato puree, rosemary, balsamic vinegar and 140 mls stock. Mix well and return to the oven for a further 15 minutes for the Quorn pieces to cook and the flavours to blend. Season well.

3. Mix the gravy powder to a smooth paste with a little cold water. Remove the casserole from the oven and stir in the gravy powder until the mixture thickens. Add a little more hot water if the consistency becomes too thick.

METHOD FOR SHORTCRUST PASTRY

4. Sieve the flour and salt into a bowl.

5. Rub the butter or margarine into the flour until the mixture resembles fine breadcrumbs.

6. Make a well in the centre and add the water gradually, stirring with a knife until the pastry begins to bind together to form a fairly firm paste.

7. Roll out about 2 thirds of the pastry to line a deep flan dish about 8½ inches (21cm) diameter and 2½ inches (5cm) deep.

8. Tip the filling into the pastry lined flan dish and spread evenly with a fork. Moisten the pastry edges with water and roll the remaining third of pastry to fit the top. Fold the pastry over the rolling pin to lift and place on top of the pie. Trim the edges to size with a knife and flute the pastry around the edges to create a seal and make the distinctive pie crust edges. Cut a small slit in the centre of the pie to let the steam escape.

9. Brush the pie with milk or beaten egg to glaze and cook in a pre-heated oven at 190°C (375°F) or Gas mark 5 for about 30 minutes until the pie is golden brown.

Serve with seasonal vegetables, mashed potatoes and gravy.

Welsh Oggie

This is my version of the traditional Welsh Oggie. This was traditionally made with lamb. As with its equivalent of the Cornish Pasty, these were eaten by the Welsh miners, with the thick crust able to be held by dirty hands so the pasty itself remained clean.

This recipe doesn't need the thick crust, but it may be worth considering for picnics etc. This makes approximately 8-10 Oggies.

SHORTCRUST PASTRY

1lb (454g) plain flour
8oz (227g) butter or hard margarine
½ teaspoon salt
approximately 8 tablespoons cold water
milk or beaten egg to glaze pastry

FILLING

8oz (227g) Quorn mince
1 tablespoon olive oil
1 medium onion, finely chopped

2 medium carrots, grated
8oz (227g) cooked new potatoes (new potatoes remain firmer inside the pastry)
1 dessert spoon mint jelly
1 pinch each of dried thyme, basil and rosemary
11 floz (313mls) stock made with 1 vegetable stock cube and 1 teaspoon of Marmite
1 dessert spoon gravy powder
ground sea salt and ground black pepper

PASTRY METHOD

1. Sieve the flour and salt into a large mixing bowl.

2. Rub the butter or margarine into the flour until the mixture resembles fine breadcrumbs.

3. Make a well in the centre and add the cold water gradually, mixing with a knife until the pastry forms a fairly firm dough.

4. Place the pastry to one side in the fridge while the filling is made.

FILLING METHOD

5. Heat the olive oil in a large frying pan and gently fry the onions for a couple of minutes, then add the grated carrot. Stir regularly and cook until both onions and carrots are softened.

6. Mix in the Quorn mince and continue to cook for a few minutes until it has been well incorporated with the onion and carrot mixture.

7. Add the stock, potatoes (cut into cubes), herbs, mint jelly. Season with salt and pepper and mix well. Simmer for a few minutes to blend the flavours together.

8. Mix the gravy powder with a little cold water and stir into the Quorn filling. Stir well to prevent lumps forming. Add a splash more hot water if mixture becomes too thick.

9. Put filling to one side to cool a little.

10. Lightly flour the worktop and roll the pastry out onto the floured surface. Use a 7inch, 8cm diameter bowl as a guide to cut round to make the circles for the pasties. You should aim to have 8-10 circles.

11. Place approximately 1 heaped tablespoon of filling in the centre of each circle. Moisten the edges with a little water and fold one side over to meet the other, so the pasty makes a half moon shape. Press the edges together with two fingers, so the distinctive pastry crust edge is formed.

12. Lightly grease a large baking tray and place the pasties on the tray. Brush with milk or beaten egg to glaze the pastry.

13. Preheat the oven to 200°C (400°F) or Gas mark 6. Place the baking tray in the oven and cook for about 20-30 minutes until the pasties are a golden brown colour.

Serve as a main dish, buffet or picnic, with a green salad, or with fresh seasonal vegetables and potatoes.

PASTA

Lasagne

Pasta Bake with Yoghurt Topping

Cheesy No Bacon and Pasta Bake

Pasta, Leek and Mince Savoury

Tasty Tagliatelle Bake

Lasagne

This is a recipe that I feel works exceptionally well with Quorn. It is a wonderfully versatile dish that everyone loves and will always be a success.

For this dish use the Bolognese sauce from my Spaghetti Bolognese recipe on page 112 and approximately 10 pieces of lasagne.

CHEESE SAUCE

2oz (56g) plain flour
1 pint (568mls) milk
1oz (28g) polyunsaturated margarine or butter

4oz (113g) grated, extra mature cheddar cheese
ground sea salt and freshly ground black pepper
2oz (56g) grated, extra mature cheddar cheese to sprinkle on top

METHOD

1. Gently heat the milk in a separate pan or in the microwave.
2. Melt the butter or margarine in a pan, then take off the heat.
3. Mix the flour into the melted butter or margarine, stirring well to remove any lumps.
4. Place the pan back on a low heat and stir well for about a minute.
5. Remove from the heat and gradually stir in the warm milk, a little at a time, stirring all the time until the milk has been absorbed into the sauce mixture.
6. Return the pan to the heat and simmer gently for a few minutes until the sauce begins to thicken, stirring continuously.
7. If lumps appear, whisk with a balloon whisk until the sauce is smooth again.
8. Add a little more milk if mixture becomes too thick.
9. Stir in the 4oz (113g) grated cheddar cheese and take off the heat.

METHOD FOR ASSEMBLING LASAGNE

10. Grease a large 7.5cm (3 inch) deep, square or rectangular baking dish.
11. Cover the base of the dish with Bolognaise sauce, then cover with lasagne. Pour a layer of cheese sauce over the pasta.
12. Repeat these layers until all the mixture has been used, ending with a layer of cheese sauce.
13. Sprinkle the 2oz (56g) grated cheese over the top and cook in a preheated oven at 180°C (350°F) or Gas mark 4 for about 30- 40 minutes until golden brown.

Serve with salad and baked potatoes or garlic bread.

Pasta Bake with Yoghurt Topping

This is a dish full of flavour that is slightly unexpected, but makes you go back for a second helping. I actually prefer the taste of natural soya yoghurt to dairy yoghurt.

I prefer to use Mafalda Corta or wholewheat Fusilli pasta in this recipe, as they have a wonderful, firm texture which lends itself beautifully to this dish.

This recipe serves 4-6 depending on portion size.

INGREDIENTS

1 bag (300g) Quorn mince
2 tablespoons olive oil
1 red pepper, washed, deseeded and chopped
1 onion, skinned and chopped
1 clove of garlic, crushed
6oz (170g) button mushrooms, wiped with damp kitchen towel and sliced
14oz (400g) tin chopped tomatoes
1½ teaspoons cayenne pepper

¼ pint (140 mls) stock made with 1teaspoon Marmite and 2 vegetable stock cubes
1 teaspoon dried mixed herbs
ground sea salt and freshly ground black pepper
6oz (170g) Mafada Corta pasta or substitute with whole wheat Fusilli pasta
10oz (284g) natural yoghurt or natural soya yoghurt
1 egg, beaten
2oz (56g) plain flour
garnish with parsley and slices of tomato

METHOD

1. In a large frying pan, gently fry the onion, garlic and peppers in the olive oil until soft.
2. Add the mushrooms and cook, stirring well for a couple of minutes.
3. Mix in the Quorn mince, tinned tomatoes with juice, stock, herbs, and cayenne pepper.
4. Stir well and simmer gently for about 10 minutes. Season well with salt and pepper.
5. Meanwhile, cook the pasta in a pan of boiling water for about 10 minutes, until tender, but not soft. Drain well.
6. Place half the pasta in the bottom of a 1 litre (2 pint) oven proof dish. Top with half the Quorn mixture. Repeat these two layers.
7. Beat together the yoghurt, egg and flour until smooth, then pour over the Quorn mixture.
8. Bake in a preheated oven at 180°C (350°F) or Gas mark 4 for 30- 40 minutes until golden brown.

Serve with a mixed salad, dressing and either garlic bread or home made bread

Cheesy No Bacon and Pasta Bake

This is a wonderfully easy and tasty meal. It can be made the day before, stored in the fridge and cooked when needed the next day.

This recipe makes approximately 4-6 portions depending on size.

INGREDIENTS

12oz (340g) Fusilli pasta
6oz (170g) grated, strong cheddar cheese
4oz (113g) Quorn bacon, roughly chopped
6 small tomatoes, chopped (on the vine always seem to taste better)

1 pint (568mls) milk, warmed
2oz (56g) butter or margarine
2oz (56g) plain flour
ground sea salt and freshly ground black pepper

METHOD

1. Cook the pasta in boiling, salted water for about 12-15 minutes until until firm to the bite (al dente). Drain and set aside to prevent overcooking.
2. Melt the butter in a non stick saucepan over a low heat. Stir in the flour, mixing well to prevent lumps forming.
3. Cook over a low heat for about a minute, stirring continually. Remove from the heat and add the milk a little at a time, stirring constantly so no lumps can form.
4. Return to the heat and allow to simmer over a gentle heat, mixing well as the sauce thickens for a couple of minutes to prevent any lumps developing.
5. Add the Quorn bacon, tomatoes and cheese, continuing to stir over a low heat until the cheese has melted into the sauce. Season with salt and pepper.
6. Mix the pasta thoroughly into the sauce, adding a splash more milk if the mixture appears too thick.
7. Pour into an oven proof dish and cook in a preheated oven at 180°C (350°F) or Gas mark 4, for about 30-40 minutes until golden brown.

Serve with a fresh green salad or assorted vegetables.

Pasta, Leek and Mince Savoury

This is another one of these time saving, yet very tasty dishes that can be prepared quickly the day before to be cooked as needed. I prefer to use Mafalda Corta pasta as the texture, shape and appearance seem to lend itself to this dish.

This dish will serve 4-6 depending on portion size and accompaniments.

INGREDIENTS

6oz (170g) Mafalda Corta pasta or whole wheat fusilli or penne pasta
12oz (340g) leeks, sliced and washed
1 clove garlic, crushed
4oz (113g) mushrooms, wiped and chopped
1 tablespoon olive oil
¼ pint (140mls) stock made with 1½ stock cubes and 1 teaspoon Marmite
1 bag (300g) Quorn mince
2 heaped tablespoons of tomato puree

1 level teaspoon dried mixed herbs
ground sea salt and freshly ground black pepper

CHEESE SAUCE

2oz (56g) butter or margarine
2oz (56g) plain flour
1 pint (568mls) skimmed milk, warmed
4oz (113g) mature cheddar cheese, grated (for sauce)
2oz (56g) mature cheddar cheese, grated (for topping)

METHOD FOR LEEK AND MINCE MIX

1. Cook the pasta until firm to the bite (al dente) for about 12-15 minutes.

2. Gently cook the leeks and garlic in the olive oil for about 5-10 minutes until soft.

3. Add the mushrooms, stirring regularly until cooked.

4. Mix in the Quorn mince and cook until defrosted.

5. Add the tomato puree and mixed herbs. Season well and mix well together to incorporate all the ingredients.

6. Dissolve the Marmite and stock cubes in the 140mls of hot water to make the stock. Add to the Quorn mixture and stir gently over a low heat until most of the water has been absorbed..

7. Layer the base of the casserole dish with half the leek and Quorn mixture.*See overleaf for method for cheese sauce.

8. Add half the cooked pasta and cover with half the cheese sauce.

9. Continue these layers until the pasta, Quorn mixture, and the cheese sauce have all been used up.

10. Sprinkle the 2oz (56g) of the remaining cheese over the top and cook in a preheated oven at 180°C (350°F) or Gas mark 4 for 30-40 minutes until golden brown.

Method for Cheese Sauce

11. Melt the butter or margarine in a pan, add the flour, mix in and cook, stirring well for 1-2 minutes. Remove from heat. Gradually add the warmed milk and stir until smooth.

12. Simmer for 3-4 minutes stirring well to prevent lumps forming, then mix in 4oz (113g) cheese.

Serve with a green salad, baby tomatoes and freshly baked bread.

Tasty Tagliatelle Bake

This is an extremely, easy, quick and tasty bake. For those short of time, it can be made the day before and cooked when needed. My children really like this, and it is always popular when they bring friends home for tea.

This will serve 4-6 people depending on portion size and accompaniments.

INGREDIENTS

1 bag (300g) Quorn pieces
8oz (227g) diced vegetables e.g. onion,
pepper and mushroom
1 tablespoon olive oil
14oz (400g) tin of chopped tomatoes
1 tablespoon soy sauce
A few shakes Worcester sauce (a vegetarian
version of this can be found in most health
food shops)
2 tablespoons tomato puree
¼ pint (140mls) stock made with 1½
vegetable stock cubes and 1 heaped teaspoon
Marmite

1 teaspoon dried mixed herbs
ground sea salt and freshly ground black
pepper
8oz (227g) whole wheat tagliatelle

CHEESE SAUCE

1oz (28g) margarine or butter
1oz (28g) plain flour
pinch of cayenne pepper
½ pint (284mls) milk, warmed
4oz (113g) strong cheddar cheese, grated
2oz (56g) strong cheddar cheese, grated to
sprinkle over the bake

METHOD

1. In a large frying pan cook the onion and pepper in the olive oil until soft. Add the mushrooms and tinned tomatoes, stirring well to stop mixture sticking.

2. Add the Worcester sauce, soy sauce, tomato puree and mixed herbs. Mix in well.

3. Stir in the Quorn pieces and the stock.

4. Simmer for 10 minutes, adding a splash more hot water if the mixture becomes too thick and season to taste with salt and pepper.

5. Cook the tagliatelle in boiling salted water until softened, but still firm to the bite.

METHOD FOR CHEESE SAUCE

1 .Melt the margarine or butter over a low heat and blend in the flour and cayenne pepper.

2. Gradually add the milk and stir continuously until the sauce thickens. I find that if you heat the milk first, it speeds up the process and results in a smoother sauce.

3. Remove from heat and stir in the 4oz (113g) cheese. Heat over a low heat until the cheese has all melted.

4. Place half the tagliatelle in the bottom of a 2 pint oven proof casserole dish. Spoon the Quorn mixture over this and top with remaining tagliatelle.

5 Pour the cheese sauce over the top, and sprinkle over the remaining 2oz (56g) grated cheese.

6. Cook in the oven at 180°C (350°F) or Gas mark 4 for 30- 40 minutes until the topping begins to turn golden brown.

Serve with a green salad or lots of fresh vegetables..

RICE

Curry

Sweet and Sour

Baked Tomato Rice with Sausages

Quorn Pieces with Sweet Chilli Sauce

No Bacon and Mushroom Risotto

Chilli Con Carne

Goulash

Paella

Curry

This is my version of an Indian style curry. We all enjoy it as a family served with Naan bread and Mango Chutney.

This recipe serves approximately 4-6 depending on portion size.

INGREDIENTS

1 bag (300g) Quorn pieces
1 large onion, finely chopped
1 large red pepper, chopped
8oz (227g) mushrooms, wiped and chopped
2 tablespoons olive oil
1 courgette, chopped
1 clove garlic, crushed
1½ vegetable stock cubes dissolved in 5 fluid ounces (140mls) water
1 teaspoon turmeric
1 teaspoon cumin
1 teaspoon coriander

14oz (400g) tin chopped tomatoes
1 heaped tablespoon tomato puree
½ – 1 teaspoon chilli flakes, depending on taste
1 tablespoon dessicated coconut
1 tablespoon ground almonds
2 handfuls fresh spinach, washed
ground sea salt and freshly ground black pepper
basmati rice to serve
Salad and slices of lemon to garnish

N.B. Use Quorn vegan pieces and make this recipe completely vegan.

METHOD

1. Heat the olive oil in a large, thick bottomed pan and fry the onions and garlic until softened. Add the red pepper and courgette, stirring intermittently until cooked, then mix in the mushrooms and continue to cook.

2. Add the Quorn pieces, turmeric, cumin, coriander, chilli flakes, tin of chopped tomatoes, tomato puree and stock.

3. Bring to the boil, then turn the heat down to simmering point. Add the dessicated coconut and ground almonds. Season well with the salt and pepper. Mix in well and continue to simmer, stirring regularly for about 10 minutes until cooked. Add a splash of boiling water if the mixture appears too dry.

4. Tear the spinach into pieces and stir into the curry mixture until wilted.

Serve with basmati rice, garnish with salad, tomatoes and slices of lemon..

Sweet and Sour

This dish just begs to be cooked in a wok for that traditional Chinese feel. The theory behind cooking in a wok is that food is cooked lightly and quickly, and therefore more of the flavour and nutrients are sealed in.

This recipe serves 4-6 depending on portion size.

INGREDIENTS

1 bag (300g) Quorn pieces
2 carrots, thinly sliced
1 onion, thinly sliced
1 red pepper, thinly sliced
1 courgette, thinly sliced
2 tablespoons vegetable oil
15½oz (435g) can pineapple chunks in natural juice - reserve the juice

2½ fluid oz (71mls) cider vinegar
2 tablespoons soy sauce
2 tablespoons dry sherry
2 tablespoons tomato ketchup
1 vegetable stock cube
1 dessert spoon cornflour
ground sea salt and freshly ground black pepper
plain brown or white rice to serve

N.B. Use Quorn vegan pieces for a great vegan alternative.

METHOD

1. Heat the wok on medium high to high heat for at least 30 seconds until hot but not smoking, then add the vegetable oil, swirling it around the wok until the inside of the wok is coated.
   N.B. One of the main keys to successful stir-frying is preheating the wok before adding oil. Adding oil to a cold wok is a sure fire way to guarantee the cooked food will stick to the bottom of the pan.

2. Add the carrots and stir fry for a couple of minutes, then add the onion, pepper and courgette. Stir fry for about 3-4 minutes until the vegetables begin to soften.

3. Add the pineapple juice, cider vinegar, soy sauce, dry sherry, tomato ketchup and stock cube.

4. Bring to simmering point, then stir in the Quorn pieces and pineapple chunks. Cook over a low heat for about 5-10 minutes.

5. Mix the cornflour with a little cold water to a runny paste and add to the mixture, stirring constantly as the mixture thickens to prevent lumps forming. Cook gently for a further 5-10 minutes. Add a splash more hot water if the mixture becomes too thick.

'Serve with plain boiled rice, I prefer to use brown rice with this recipe'.

33

Baked Tomato Rice with Sausages

This is an extremely tasty, quick and versatile meal that can be prepared in advance and cooked when required. It is a great favourite with kids, and is one of those recipes that you use time and time again.

This serves 4-6 people depending on portion size and accompaniments.

INGREDIENTS

1 onion, finely chopped
1 red pepper, chopped
2 garlic cloves, finely crushed or chopped
2 tablespoons olive oil
½ teaspoon dried thyme
10oz (284g) arborio/ risotto rice
1¾ pints (1 litre) vegetable stock made with 2 vegetable stock cubes
14oz (400g) tin chopped tomatoes

1 tablespoon tomato puree
1 bay leaf
1 teaspoon dried basil
6oz (170g) grated mature cheddar cheese
2 tablespoons chopped chives
1 packet of 8 Quorn sausages, defrosted and cut into slices
2-3 tablespoons grated parmesan cheese or mature cheddar cheese
ground sea salt and freshly ground black pepper

METHOD

1. Heat the oil in a large pan or wok. Add the onion and pepper, and cook, stirring well until soft.
2. Stir in the garlic and thyme and cook for a further minute.
3. Add the rice and cook stirring frequently for about 2 minutes. Add the stock, tin of tomatoes, tomato puree, bay leaf and sausages. Season well with the salt and pepper.
4. Simmer gently for about 5-10 minutes, stirring frequently until most of the stock has been absorbed.
5. Mix in the basil, cheddar cheese and chives. Tip into an oven proof casserole dish and cover with the lid.
6. Bake in a preheated oven at 180°C (350°F) or Gas mark 4 for 30 minutes.
7. Sprinkle with parmesan cheese or grated mature cheddar cheese and return to the oven for a further 5-10 minutes without the lid, until the top is golden and bubbling.
8. N.B. If making in advance, store in the refrigerator until ready to be cooked.

Serve with a mixed green salad and freshly baked bread.

Quorn Pieces with Sweet Chilli Sauce

This is a chilli recipe that appeals more to children and adults who aren't keen on hot, spicy chillies, such as Chilli-con-Carne etc. This recipe is best made the day before and refrigerated, as this allows the flavours to develop and infuse into the ingredients.

This recipe will make approximately 4-6 servings, depending on portion size.

INGREDIENTS

1 medium onion, finely chopped
1 clove garlic, crushed
2 tablespoons olive oil
1 green and 1 red pepper, finely chopped
6oz (170g) mushrooms, wiped and chopped
1 bag (300g) Quorn pieces
1½ stock cubes
14oz (400g) tin chopped tomatoes
2 tablespoons tomato puree
2oz (56g) sugar

2 fluid oz (57mls) cider vinegar
ground sea salt and freshly ground black pepper
1 level teaspoon cinnamon
½ teaspoon ground mixed spice
1 teaspoon chilli powder
rice to serve
freshly chopped tomatoes, onion and cucumber to garnish

N.B. Use Quorn vegan pieces for a great vegan alternative.

METHOD

1. Fry the onions, garlic and peppers in the olive oil until softened. Add the mushrooms and continue to cook for a couple more minutes.
2. Add the tinned tomatoes, tomato puree, cinnamon, mixed spice, cider vinegar, sugar, chilli powder and stock cubes.
3. Gently bring to simmering point, stirring well to prevent the sugar from sticking.
4. Add the Quorn pieces and mix well into the sauce. Season well with salt and pepper.
5. Simmer for about 10-15 minutes to cook through. Add a splash of hot water if mixture becomes too thick.

Serve with plain boiled rice, I prefer to use brown rice with this recipe.

No Bacon and Mushroom Risotto

This is one of my favourite, quick, go to meals. It can be prepared the morning or the night before. It is easy to prepare, but still satisfying and full of flavour. I love this dish served with grilled tomatoes.

This recipe will make approximately 4-6 servings depending on portion size.

INGREDIENTS

1 large onion, finely chopped
2 cloves garlic, crushed
1 tablespoon olive oil
10oz (284g) mix of mushrooms eg. chestnut and field mushrooms, wiped and chopped
1 glass dry white wine
10oz (284g) aborio/risotto rice
5 slices Quorn bacon, chopped

1 teaspoon dried mixed herbs
1½ pints (900mls) stock made with 2 vegetable stock cubes
1 dessert spoon mushroom ketchup
ground sea salt and freshly ground black pepper
2oz (56g) parmesan or grated extra mature cheddar cheese
chopped parsley

METHOD

1. Heat the oil in a large non stick pan and gently fry the onion and garlic until soft.
2. Add the mushrooms and continue to fry over a low heat until cooked.
3. Pour in the white wine. Add the mushroom ketchup, Quorn bacon and mixed herbs, stirring well into the onion and mushroom mixture. Cook for about 5 minutes.
4. Mix the rice in well to absorb the flavours.
5. Add the stock, stir well and bring to boiling point. Season well with salt and pepper.
6. Turn down the heat and simmer gently for approximately 10-15 minutes until most of the stock has been absorbed by the rice. Add a splash more water if the mixture looks like it is becoming too dry. The rice should be 'al dente' which means firm to the bite.
7. Sprinkle with grated extra mature cheddar cheese or parmesan cheese and chopped parsley to serve.
8. N.B. Store in the refrigerator until ready to be reheated if making in advance.

Serve with a fresh green salad and vine tomatoes, or on its own with grilled tomatoes.

Chilli Con Carne

This recipe provides a tasty and quick alternative to the traditional meat dish. With its spicy edge and rich flavour, it is a firm favourite amongst our family and friends.

It makes a perfect family meal that can be easily made the day before, which only serves to improve the flavour.

Chilli Con Carne also lends itself well to those less formal evenings with a group of good friends and a couple of bottles of red wine. Again, it can be made the day before, stored in the refrigerator and reheated as required. Simply increase the recipe as needed for the number of guests, and serve with plain boiled rice. You could also add some mixed salad bowls and an assortment of dressings.

The amusing part is to sit back and let the guests comment on the food and realise that no one has any idea that it is a Quorn Chilli and doesn't contain any meat at all.

This recipe will make approximately 4-6 servings depending on portion sizes.

INGREDIENTS

1 bag (300g) Quorn mince
1 onion, chopped
1 red pepper, deseeded and chopped
2 tablespoons olive oil
1 large clove garlic, crushed
14oz (400g) tin chopped tomatoes
9oz (255g) passata
14oz (400g) tin kidney beans, drained

4 fluid oz (114mls) stock made with 1 vegetable stock cube
1 teaspoon chilli powder
1 teaspoon ground cumin
½ teaspoon paprika powder
2 tablespoons tomato puree
1 heaped teaspoon Marmite
1 dessert spoon gravy powder
ground sea salt and freshly ground black pepper

METHOD

1. Heat the oil in a pan. Add the onion, garlic and pepper and cook until softened, stirring regularly.

2. Add the Quorn mince, tin of tomatoes, passata, tomato puree, chilli powder, ground cumin and paprika powder.

3. Drain the tin of kidney beans and add to mixture.

4. Add the stock, Marmite, then season well with salt and pepper. Mix well, bring to the boil and gently simmer for about 10 minutes.

5. Mix the gravy powder to a pouring consistency with a little cold water and add to the

Quorn mixture, stirring continuously until the mixture thickens. Add a splash more boiling water if the consistency becomes too thick.

Serve with boiled white or brown rice.

Goulash

This is my version of this famous Hungarian dish. I personally love it, and have had nothing but praise when I have served it up to friends and family.

This recipe will make approximately 4-6 helpings depending on portion size.

INGREDIENTS

1 bag (300g) Quorn pieces
2 medium onions, skinned and chopped
1 green pepper, deseeded and chopped
6oz (170g) mushrooms, wiped with damp kitchen towel and chopped
2 tablespoons olive oil
1 level teaspoon paprika
1 heaped teaspoon Marmite
3 level tablespoons tomato puree

pinch grated nutmeg
2 large tomatoes, skinned and chopped
1 Bouquet Garni
½ pint (284mls) stock made up with 1 vegetable stock cube
5 fluid oz (140mls) soured cream
ground sea salt and freshly ground black pepper
rice to serve
chopped parsley to garnish

METHOD

1. Fry the onions, garlic and pepper in the olive oil in a large pan or skillet until soft, stirring regularly to prevent sticking.

2. Add the mushrooms and chopped tomatoes then continue to cook until softened.

3. Add the Quorn pieces and cook for a few minutes until thoroughly defrosted.

4. Stir in the tomato puree, nutmeg, paprika, stock, Marmite and bouquet garni. Season well with salt and pepper.

5. Turn into an oven proof casserole dish and cook in a preheated oven at 180°C (350°F) or Gas mark 4 for 30-40 minutes. Add a splash more boiling water if the mixture becomes too thick.

6. Before serving, stir in the soured cream.

Serve with boiled rice and sprinkle chopped parsley over the top to garnish.

43

Paella

This is my version of a Spanish Paella. Traditionally, it is made with prawns and various sea food as well as a variety of different types of meat. It is extremely easy to make and is very tasty.

This recipe serves approximately 4-6 people depending on portion size.

INGREDIENTS

1 red onion, chopped

1 red pepper and 1 green pepper, deseeded and chopped

1 garlic clove, crushed

6oz (170g) mushrooms, wiped with damp kitchen towel and chopped

2 tablespoons olive oil

3 Quorn gammon steaks

12oz (340g) paella rice

1¾ pints (1 litre) stock made with 2 vegetable stock cubes

14oz (400g) tin chopped tomatoes

juice of ½ lemon

3 tablespoons dry sherry

1 tablespoon tomato puree

1 teaspoon hot smoked paprika

1 teaspoon dried thyme

5oz (142g) dwarf green beans

ground sea salt and freshly ground black pepper

tomatoes, salad, lemon slices and chopped parsley to garnish

METHOD

1. Heat the oil in a large pan. Add the onion, peppers and garlic and fry gently until soft.

2. Add the rice and cook, stirring well for a couple of minutes. Pour in the stock and the tin of tomatoes. This does seem like a lot of liquid initially, but it will quickly be absorbed into the rice. Bring to the boil, then turn down to simmering point, stirring regularly. The rice will take approximately 10-15 minutes in total to cook.

3. While the rice is cooking, place the Quorn gammon steaks under the grill and cook for about 5 minutes on each side until lightly cooked. Cut into small chunks and add to the rice mixture.

4. Add the remaining ingredients and continue to cook very gently until the rice is cooked. Be careful at this stage as the rice will begin to stick to the pan and therefore needs careful mixing.

5. Keep testing to see if the rice is cooked. Visually it will have become larger in size and look softer. It should be as the chefs say, 'Firm to the bite'. You may need to add a little more liquid if the mixture becomes too dry. Once cooked, transfer into a serving dish.

Serve with a green salad and garnish with chopped parsley.

EASY SUPPER

Fajitas

Tasty Bites

Pumpkin Stew

Crunchy Onion Bake

Mushroom Stroganoff with Yoghurt

Roasted Mediterranean Vegetables with Cous Cous

Sweet Potato and Quorn Bacon Frittata Muffins

Gnocchi with a Simple Tomato Sauce

Quorn Pieces with Mushroom Sauce

No Beef and Onions in Stout

Mushroom Stroganoff

Beefless Burgers

Fajitas

These Mexican style wraps are extremely versatile and can be used in many different ways.

They can provide a tasty accompaniment to a buffet, they can be served as a light lunch, or with a salad for a more filling meal. However they are served, they are delicious, packed full of spicy flavours.

This recipe will make approximately 4-6 Fajitas depending on portion size.

INGREDIENTS

1 bag (312g) Quorn fillets defrosted and cut into strips or 300g bag frozen Quorn Pieces
1 tablespoon olive oil
1 onion, thinly sliced
1 red pepper, thinly sliced
1 green pepper, thinly sliced
2-3 teaspoons of Mexican Fajita or Taco seasoning

pinch of dried chilli flakes (optional extra)
1 pack Mexican Tortilla wraps
4oz (113g) grated, strong cheddar cheese
ground sea salt and freshly ground black pepper
sour cream, salsa or guacamole to serve

N.B. If you like your food to be spicy, add the extra pinch of dried chilli flakes to method number 3.

METHOD

1. Heat the oil in a large frying pan or wok and gently fry the onion and peppers until soft.
2. Add the Quorn and toss for a few minutes in the oil with the onions and peppers.
3. Add the Fajita or Taco seasoning and cook for about 5-10 minutes, stirring well to incorporate the flavours and cook the Quorn through. Season well with salt and pepper.
4. Cook the tortillas as instructed on the packaging.
5. Pace a large spoon of the Quorn and vegetable mixture in the centre of each tortilla and sprinkle grated cheese over the filling. Roll the tortilla around the filling and serve immediately.

Serve with sour cream, salsa or guacamole
according to taste.

Tasty Bites

These are extremely tasty and versatile. They can be served with virtually anything, but also make a delicious breakfast alternative. Tasty Bites can be made in advance the day before and refrigerated until they are ready to be cooked.

This recipe makes approximately 8 -10 Bites depending on size.

INGREDIENTS

½ bag (150g) Quorn mince
4 fluid oz (114mls) stock made with 1
teaspoon Marmite and 1 vegetable stock cube
1lb (454g) potatoes, peeled and quartered
1oz (28g) margarine or butter
2oz (56g) strong cheddar cheese, grated

1 dessert spoon Worcester sauce (a vegetarian version of this is available in most health food shops)
½ teaspoon dried rosemary
ground sea salt and freshly ground black pepper
1 egg, beaten
breadcrumbs or sesame seeds for coating

METHOD

1. Cook the potatoes in boiling salted water until soft, drain and mash with butter or margarine.
2. Put the Quorn mince into a pan with the 113mls of stock. Add the Worcester sauce, rosemary and season with salt and pepper. Heat gently for a couple of minutes, stirring well to prevent it sticking.
3. Blend the Quorn mixture in a food processor or blender until smooth in texture.
4. In a bowl, mix the potato and cheese into the Quorn mixture, add the egg and stir well.
5. Lightly coat hands with flour and mould the mixture into balls, using about a tablespoon of the Quorn mixture for each ball.
6. Roll the balls in either sesame seeds or breadcrumbs until well coated, then flatten the balls, so a burger type shape is produced.
7. Place on a greased baking tray and cook in a pre-heated oven 190°C (375°F) or Gas mark 5, for 20-30 minutes turning once halfway through cooking time.
8. Alternatively, place under a low/ medium grill for about 10 minutes on each side.

Try serving piping hot, with home made chutney, grilled tomatoes, mushrooms and baked beans, or with baked potato and salad.

Pumpkin Stew

I created this stew by default, after my daughter brought home a pumpkin she had grown in the gardening club at school. I had never actually tried this member of the squash family before.

We were all surprised how tasty this dish was, and how well the slight sweetness of the pumpkin complimented the other flavours.

This recipe will make approximately 4-6 servings depending on portion size.

INGREDIENTS

1 onion, finely chopped
2 tablespoons olive oil
1lb (454g) pumpkin, skinned and de seeded
1 bag (300g) Quorn pieces
1 teaspoon dried mixed herbs
1 teaspoon Marmite

1 pint (568mls) stock made with 2 vegetable stock cubes
ground sea salt and freshly ground black pepper
1 dessert spoon gravy powder

N.B. Use Quorn vegan pieces to make this recipe a great vegan alternative.

METHOD

1. Heat the oil in a frying pan and gently fry the onion until soft.
2. Cut the pumpkin into approximately 1 inch (2.5cm) cubes and put into a large oven proof casserole dish.
3. Tip the cooked onion and juices into the casserole dish with the mixed herbs, Marmite, stock, Quorn pieces and season well with salt and pepper. Mix all the ingredients together thoroughly.
4. Cook in a preheated oven at 180°C (350°F) or Gas mark 4 for about 30-40 minutes, until the pumpkin has softened.
5. Mix the gravy powder to a smooth paste with a little water and add to the stew. Stir well to prevent lumps forming as the gravy begins to thicken. Add a little extra hot water if the mixture becomes too thick.
6. Return to the oven for a further 10 minutes, mix well before serving.

Serve with roast potatoes and fresh seasonal vegetables.

Crunchy Onion Bake

I personally love this recipe. The onion sauce topping really enhances the flavour of the dish. I find that using dried onions in the sauce gives a better flavour, but you could easily use a fresh onion if you preferred.

INGREDIENTS

2 medium onions, chopped

2 medium carrots, grated

2 sticks celery, washed and chopped

1 bag (300g) Quorn mince

2 tablespoons olive oil

1oz (28g) wholemeal flour

¾ pint (424mls) vegetable stock made with 1 vegetable stock cube and 1 teaspoon Marmite

1 teaspoon dried mixed herbs

ground sea salt and freshly ground black pepper

1oz (28g) wholemeal breadcrumbs

ONION SAUCE

1oz (28g) vegetable margarine or butter

1oz (28g) plain flour

½ pint (284mls) milk, warmed

¼ teaspoon onion salt

1 level tablespoon dried, chopped onion

METHOD

1. Heat the oil in a large frying pan and gently cook the onion, carrot and celery for a few minutes until softened.

2. Blend in the flour and cook for 1 minute stirring continuously. Add the stock gradually, mixing all the time to prevent lumps forming. Bring to the boil, then turn down the heat and simmer gently for a further 2 minutes, still stirring.

3. Add the Quorn mince to the onion and vegetables and mix together thoroughly. Simmer gently for 5-10 minutes. Add a splash of hot water if mixture becomes too thick.

4. Season well with salt and pepper.

METHOD FOR ONION SAUCE

5. Melt the margarine or butter over a low heat, blend in the flour to form a thick paste, and pour in the milk, stirring continuously. I find this process much easier if you heat the milk first, as it thickens more quickly and therefore the sauce is less likely to stick and burn.

6. Stir until thickened, mix in the onion salt, dried onion and remove from the heat.

7. Put half the Quorn mixture into an oven proof casserole dish, then pour half the sauce over it. Repeat these two layers. Sprinkle breadcrumbs over the top.

8. Bake at 180°C (350°F) or Gas mark 4 for about 30 minutes, until the topping is golden brown.

Serve with a selection of roasted vegetables and grilled tomatoes.

Mushroom Stroganoff with Yoghurt

This recipe brings a refreshing tasty alternative to the traditional recipe. Again, I prefer the taste of natural soya yoghurt to dairy yoghurt in this recipe, which makes this an ideal alternative for a vegan menu.

It is a relatively straight forward dish which can easily be prepared the day before and refrigerated. It is best served, as in its traditional form, with plain boiled rice.

This is a meal that will impress the vegans and meat eaters alike.

INGREDIENTS

1 bag (300g) Quorn pieces
1 large onion, skinned and chopped
2 tablespoons olive oil
10oz (284g) button mushrooms
1 large clove garlic, crushed
½ teaspoon ground nutmeg
1 teaspoon dried mixed herbs
1 dessert spoon mushroom ketchup
¼ pint (140mls) stock made with 2 vegetable stock cubes

¼ pint (140mls) unsweetened soya or oat milk.
2 dessert spoons cornflour
4oz (113g) natural soya yoghurt
ground sea salt and freshly ground black pepper
plain boiled rice to serve
chopped parsley to garnish

N.B. Use Quorn vegan pieces to make this recipe a great vegan alternative.

METHOD

1. In a large frying pan, gently cook the onion and garlic in the olive oil until softened. Add the mushrooms, mix well and continue to fry until cooked.
2. Add the Quorn pieces and cook, stirring well for a few minutes until defrosted and softened.
3. Add the stock, milk, nutmeg, mixed herbs and mushroom ketchup, then season well with salt and pepper to taste. Bring to simmering point very gently.
4. Mix the cornflour to a paste with a little milk and add to the Quorn mixture, stirring continually until it begins to thicken.
5. Simmer gently for about 5-10 minutes, stirring regularly. Add a splash more milk if the mixture becomes too thick.
6. Stir in the yoghurt and bring back to simmering point until it is heated through.

Serve piping hot with plain boiled rice and garnish with chopped parsley and a sprinkle of cayenne pepper.

Roasted Mediterranean Vegetables with Couscous

This is a dish full of Mediterranean flavours that combine together to create a meal that asks for a good bottle of red wine to accompany it, and a breath taking view over a balcony to finish it.

This recipe serves 4-6 people depending on portion size.

INGREDIENTS

1 bag (300g) Quorn pieces
1 small red, green and yellow pepper, washed and sliced
1 onion, peeled and sliced
1 courgette, washed and sliced
1 teaspoon chilli flakes
2 -3 tablespoons olive oil
6 fluid oz (170mls) stock made with 1 vegetable stock cube and 1 level teaspoon Marmite
pinch of rosemary
pinch of thyme

1 dessert spoon mint jelly
½ tablespoon finely chopped parsley
ground sea salt and freshly ground black pepper

COUSCOUS

Allow 2oz, (56g) per person
1 dessert spoon chopped parsley
1oz (28g) butter or vegan margarine
ground sea salt and freshly ground black pepper

N.B. Use Quorn vegan pieces to make this meal a great vegan alternative.

METHOD

1. Spread the peppers, onion, and courgette in the base of an oven proof baking dish. Sprinkle with the olive oil, season well with salt and pepper and place in a preheated oven 220°C (425°F) or Gas mark 7 for 15-20 minutes, until the vegetables begin to soften. Turn halfway through the cooking time.

2. In a separate pan, mix the Quorn pieces with the 6 fluid oz (170ml) stock, mint jelly, pinch of thyme, rosemary, chilli flakes and ½ tablespoon chopped parsley. Cook over a low heat for about 5 minutes until most of the liquid and flavour has been absorbed into the Quorn pieces. Season to taste with salt and pepper.

3. Take the vegetables out of the oven, mix well, then add the Quorn mixture. Turn the oven down to 180°C (350°F) or Gas mark 4. Stir well to incorporate the ingredients and return to the oven for a further 15 minutes.

4. Prepare the Couscous as per instructions on the packet. A rough guide is to add ½ pint (284mls) boiling water to every 4oz (113g) Couscous. Stir, then bring to the boil.

Remove from heat, stir in 1 dessert spoon of chopped parsley and 1oz (28g) butter or margarine, cover with a lid and leave to stand for 5 minutes.

5. Serve the Couscous in a circle on each plate and place a large spoon of the vegetable and Quorn mixture in the centre.

Serve with a fresh green salad and dressing.

Sweet Potato and Quorn Bacon Frittata Muffins

This is a meal that is high in protein and low in carbohydrates.

Cooked in muffin cases, these can be eaten hot or cold, as part of a meal, or as a protein filled snack.

This makes approximately 6-8 muffins depending on size.

INGREDIENTS

4 rashers of Quorn bacon, chopped
1 sweet potato, peeled and grated
1 courgette, topped, tailed and grated
1 onion, finely chopped

1 tablespoon olive oil
4 eggs
4oz (113g) mature cheddar cheese, grated.
ground sea salt and freshly ground black pepper

METHOD

1. Peel and grate the sweet potato. Wash well before grating.
2. Top, tail and wash the courgette before grating.
3. Fry the onion in the olive oil on a low heat until softened. Add the grated sweet potato and courgette, stir well. Cover with a lid and cook on a low heat for about 5 minutes until soft. Take off the heat.
4. Beat the 4 eggs into a bowl and season with salt and pepper.
5. Pour the eggs, chopped Quorn bacon and grated cheese into the vegetable mixture and stir well. Season to taste with salt and pepper.
6. Using a spoon, fill each paper muffin case with the mixture and place on a oven proof tray or a muffin tray.
7. Cook at 200°C (400°F) or Gas mark 6 for 15 minutes or until firm and lightly browned.

Serve with a green salad.

Gnocchi with a Simple Tomato Sauce

This is a very simple tomato sauce recipe that works really well when served on a bed of gnocchi, with grated Parmesan cheese sprinkled over the top.

Gnocchi is a great alternative to pasta. Gnocchi will cook in about 5 minutes which makes this an incredibly quick but nutritious meal to prepare. Beware that gnocchi is extremely filling, but is very well suited to this simple sauce.

This recipe will give 4-6 servings depending on portion size.

INGREDIENTS

1 bag (300g) Quorn pieces
1 medium to large onion, finely chopped
2 cloves garlic, crushed
2 tablespoons olive oil
3 tablespoons tomato puree
1 heaped teaspoon dried oregano
1 teaspoon dried basil
14oz (400g) tin of chopped tomatoes

¼ pint (140mls) stock made with 2 stock cubes
ground sea salt and freshly ground black pepper
gnocchi to serve, serving sizes as per packet instructions.
parmesan cheese to sprinkle on top
basil leaves to garnish

N.B. Use Quorn vegan pieces and omit the parmesan cheese or replace with vegan cheese if a vegan meal is required.

METHOD

1. Heat the olive oil in a large pan and gently fry the onion and garlic until softened.
2. Add the Quorn pieces and fry with the onion and garlic mixture for a couple of minutes until thoroughly defrosted.
3. Mix the tinned tomatoes in with the onion and Quorn mixture.
4. Add the tomato puree, dried herbs, stock and sugar. Bring to boiling point, stirring well and continue to simmer over a very low heat for 10 minutes
5. Add a splash more hot water if the sauce becomes too thick. Season with salt and pepper.
6. To cook the gnocchi, bring a pan of salted water to the boil, add the gnocchi and simmer for 5 minutes until soft but not falling apart.

Serve the sauce on a bed of gnocchi, with freshly grated parmesan cheese and garnish with basil leaves.

Quorn Pieces with Mushroom Sauce

This is quite a rich dish, though very tasty. The mushroom ketchup, (found in large supermarkets and delicatessens) really adds to the flavour. This can be made with either Quorn pieces or fillets.

This recipe will provide approximately 4-6 servings depending on portion size.

INGREDIENTS

1 bag (300g) Quorn pieces or 1 bag (312g) of Quorn fillets
2 tablespoons olive oil
1 medium to large onion, finely chopped
12oz (340g) mushrooms, wiped and sliced
1 clove garlic, crushed
4 fluid oz (113mls) stock made with 1 vegetable stock cube
1 glass white wine

1 dessert spoon mushroom ketchup
1 teaspoon dried mixed herbs
¼ teaspoon cayenne pepper
1 level dessert spoon cornflour
milk to mix cornflour paste
ground sea salt and freshly ground black pepper
2 tablespoons of chopped parsley to garnish

N.B. If using Quorn Fillets, they will need to be defrosted before use and cooked under the grill.

METHOD

1. Heat the olive oil in a large pan and gently cook the onion and garlic over a low heat until softened. Add the mushrooms, stirring well until cooked.

2. Mix the Quorn pieces into the mushroom mixture and continue to cook for a few minutes.

3. If using Quorn fillets, put them under the grill to cook. Turn regularly so they are evenly cooked on both sides.

4. Add the wine, herbs, cayenne pepper, mushroom ketchup and stock to the mushroom mixture. Season well with salt and pepper. Bring to boiling point and simmer gently for about 10 minutes.

5. Mix the dessert spoon of cornflour with a little milk to a smooth paste and gradually stir into the mushroom mixture, stirring well as the sauce begins to thicken, to prevent lumps forming. Add a little more hot water if the sauce becomes too thick.

6. If using the Quorn fillets, plate them up in a large serving dish, or on individual plates and pour the mushroom sauce over the top.

7. Garnish with chopped parsley and serve immediately with plenty of fresh vegetables.

This dish works well with a plate of roasted vegetables fresh from the oven.

No Beef and Onions in Stout

This is extremely quick and easy to make. It can be made the day or morning before and refrigerated until needed.

This recipe will make approximately 4-6 servings depending on portion size.

INGREDIENTS

1 bag (300g) Quorn pieces
2 tablespoons olive oil
2 large onions, thinly sliced
8oz (227g) mushrooms, wiped with damp kitchen towel and sliced
1 teaspoon dried mixed herbs
¼ pint (140mls) stout

¾ pint (424mls) stock made with 2 vegetable stock cubes and 1 teaspoon Marmite
1 teaspoon Worcester sauce. A vegetarian version of this can be bought in most health food shops.
1 dessert spoon gravy powder
ground sea salt and freshly ground black pepper

METHOD

1. Heat the oil in a large pan and gently fry the onions until softened. Add the mushrooms and continue to cook stirring regularly for a few minutes.

2. Add the Quorn pieces, mixed herbs, stout, Worcester sauce, stock, and season with salt and pepper.

3. Bring to boiling point and simmer for about 10 minutes.

4. Transfer the mixture to a large oven proof casserole dish and cook in a preheated oven at 180°C (350°F) or Gas mark 4 for 30 minutes.

5. Remove from the oven. Mix the gravy powder to a smooth paste with a little cold water and pour into the casserole stirring well to prevent lumps forming. Add a splash more hot water if the mixture becomes too thick.

6. Return to the oven for a further 10 minutes, stir well and serve.

Serve with roast potatoes, fresh seasonal vegetables
and lashings of gravy.

Mushroom Stroganoff

This is a really delicious dish that is perfect for a small intimate dinner party with friends. It is deceptively quick and easy to make, and will appeal to most tastes.

This recipe will provide 4-6 servings depending on portion size.

INGREDIENTS

1 bag (300g) Quorn pieces
1 large onion, finely chopped
1 clove garlic, crushed
2 tablespoons olive oil
12oz (340g) mushrooms, wiped with damp kitchen towel and sliced
1 tablespoon mushroom ketchup (this is found in most large supermarkets and delicatessens)

½ teaspoon ground nutmeg
¼ pint (140mls) stock made with 2 vegetable stock cubes
4 fluid oz (114ml) soured cream
ground sea salt and freshly ground black pepper
plain boiled rice to serve
2 tablespoons chopped parsley
1 teaspoon caraway seeds (optional)

METHOD

1. Heat the olive oil in a large frying pan and fry the onions and garlic gently over a low heat until soft.
2. Mix in the mushrooms and continue to fry for a few minutes.
3. Stir in the Quorn pieces.
4. Add the stock, mushroom ketchup and nutmeg. Season with salt and pepper.
5. Simmer gently for about 10 minutes, stirring well until the Quorn is soft and cooked through.
6. If the mixture appears too dry, add a splash of boiling water.
7. Stir in the soured cream over a low heat until it has heated through.

Serve immediately with plain boiled rice and garnish with chopped parsley and caraway seeds.

Beefless Burgers

This recipe book would not be complete without my version of the classic 'Beefburger'. This loses none of the taste, is a much healthier version, but still retains that fast food commodity we all crave occasionally.

The crux of this recipe is not to scrimp on the meat like flavours which is why I have used a stock cube and a stock pot. These are usually found together in most supermarkets.

This recipe makes approximately 10 burgers depending on size. They can be made the day before, and stored in the refrigerator.

INGREDIENTS

1 large bag (500g) Quorn mince
1 medium red onion, finely chopped
2 shallots, finely chopped
2 cloves garlic, crushed
4 tablespoons olive oil
1 heaped teaspoon Marmite
1 dessert spoon gravy powder

2 teaspoons smoked paprika
1 vegetable stock cube
1 vegetable stock pot
5 fluid oz (140mls) boiling water
3oz (85g) brown breadcrumbs
1 egg, beaten
ground sea salt and ground black pepper.
plain flour to shape the burgers

METHOD

1. Gently fry the onion, shallots and garlic in the olive oil until softened.

2. In a separate pan, dissolve the Marmite, stock cube and vegetable stock pot in 100mls of the boiling water. Add the Quorn mince and mix well over a low heat for a couple of minutes until all the liquid has been absorbed.

3. Stir in the smoked paprika and season well with sea salt and ground black pepper.

4. Blend the Quorn mixture in a food processor or blender until smooth and return to the pan. Sprinkle small amounts of the gravy powder over the Quorn, stirring well before adding any more. Add the last 40mls hot water. Turn the heat back on low and mix thoroughly to prevent lumps forming. Turn off the heat.

5. Add the cooked onion, garlic and breadcrumbs and mix thoroughly into the Quorn mixture.

6. Beat the eggs and mix well into the ingredients.

7. Coat the hands with flour. Use a heaped tablespoon to measure the approximate size of mixture, shape into burgers and place onto a greased baking tray ready for cooking. Makes approximately 10 burgers.

8. Heat 2 tablespoons oil in a large frying pan and cook the burgers over a low heat,

turning regularly to ensure they are evenly cooked and brown on both sides. Continue until all burgers are cooked, using extra oil as necessary.

Serve in a bun with salad, relish,
sweet potato chips and enjoy.

ONE POTS & STEWS

Irish Stew

Bakers Casserole

Aubergine Surprise

Sausage and Cider Stew

Sausage and Leek Hotpot

Cheese and No Bacon Pie

Leek and Mushroom Casserole with Cider Sauce

Thyme Hot pot with Crispy Dumplings

Herby Vegetable Casserole

Honeyed Stew

Cottage Pie

Irish Stew

This is my version of this well known dish. It is traditionally made with mutton and root vegetables which were the staple Irish diet many years ago.

I have added Guinness to the recipe as it seemed to cry out for it, but beware, Guinness needs to be well cooked to remove any bitterness in flavour.

This stew tastes wonderful. It is full of texture and taste, and benefits in its flavour from being made the day before and refrigerated over night.

This stew will serve 4-6 people depending on portion size and accompaniments.

INGREDIENTS

1 bag (300g) Quorn pieces
1lb (454g) onions, peeled and sliced thinly
11oz (312g) carrots, sliced
1 medium parsnip, sliced
11oz (312g) potatoes, peeled and sliced
1 tablespoon pearl barley
2 garlic cloves, crushed
1 bay leaf
1 teaspoon dried thyme or a sprig of fresh thyme

1 level dessert spoon gravy powder
1 level dessert spoon cornflour
¾ pint (424mls) Guinness made up to 1½ pints (852mls) with vegetable stock, made with 2 vegetable stock cubes and 1 teaspoon of Marmite
2 good shakes Worcester sauce (a vegetarian version of this is available from most health food shops)
sea salt and freshly ground black pepper

METHOD

1. Put onions, carrots, parsnip, potatoes, pearl barley, garlic, bay leaf, Worcestershire sauce, Guinness and stock into a large casserole dish and season well with salt and pepper.

2. Cook in a pre-heated oven at 180°C (350°F) or Gas mark 4 for one hour.

3. Remove from the oven and add the Quorn pieces and thyme. Stir well and return to the oven for a further half hour.

4. Blend the gravy powder and cornflour to a custard type consistency with about 50mls of water, lift the stew out of the oven, and pour the gravy mix into the stew, stirring continually as the mixture thickens to prevent lumps forming. Add a splash more hot water if the mixture becomes too thick. Return to the oven for a further 15 minutes, or until the vegetables have cooked.

5. You may need to add a little more boiling water at this stage to prevent the stew over thickening. It should have a gravy like consistency.

Serve with potatoes, fresh vegetables and gravy.

Baker's Casserole

This recipe is inspired by the importance of the bakehouse in village life in rural Greek and Cypriot villages. Each village had a communal oven where the villagers used to take their casseroles to be cooked at the end of the day. It provided a sense of community, a place where the women could meet and chat.

There are still some parts of Greece where on special occasions, villagers take their dishes to the village baker to be cooked in the bread oven.

Traditionally, these casseroles could be made all year round with an endless variety of meat, vegetables and spices depending on the seasonal availability of different produce.

My version is extremely tasty, rich in flavour, and yet manages to maintain a totally original taste. Try it, you won't be disappointed.

This will serve 4-6 people depending on portion sizes.

INGREDIENTS

1 bag (312g) Quorn Fillets
2 medium onions, thinly sliced
1 clove garlic, crushed
2 tablespoons olive oil
6oz (170g) dwarf or green beans with the ends cut off
12oz (340g) fresh tomatoes, peeled and chopped
1 heaped tablespoon tomato puree

1 teaspoon honey
1 teaspoon lemon juice
1 teaspoon cumin
1 heaped teaspoon oregano
1½ pint (852mls) stock made with 2 vegetable stock cubes and 1 teaspoon Marmite
1 level tablespoon gravy powder
ground sea salt and freshly ground black pepper

METHOD

1. In a large pan, heat the oil and gently fry the onions and garlic until softened. Add the tomatoes and allow to cook for a few minutes, stirring as needed.
2. Add the tomato puree, honey, lemon juice, cumin, oregano and stock. Season well with salt and freshly ground black pepper and bring to simmering point, stirring regularly.
3. Add the Quorn fillets and the dwarf beans. Turn the heat down to low and allow to cook for about 5 minutes to infuse the flavour into the Quorn.
4. Transfer the Baker's Casserole into an oven proof casserole dish and bake in a preheated oven at 180°C (350°F) or Gas mark 4 for 30 minutes.

5. Remove from the oven. Mix the gravy powder to a smooth paste and pour into the casserole stirring constantly as the gravy thickens to prevent lumps forming. You may need to add a splash of hot water from the kettle if the gravy appears too thick.

6. Return to the oven for an extra 10 minutes to heat through and ensure the casserole is piping hot before serving.

Serve with seasonal vegetables and potatoes.

Aubergine Surprise

This dish provides a rather interesting combination of Aubergines and natural yoghurt. I actually prefer the taste of Soya yoghurt in this recipe, which does give the option of a vegan alternative if the grated cheese and eggs are removed. In this case, the soya yoghurt could be used on its own as a topping.

Aubergines are one of those hit and miss vegetables that people seldom do right and then never try again. The trick with aubergines is to salt them well. This removes that bitter edge and tenderises them.

This recipe will serve 4-6 people depending on portion size.

INGREDIENTS

1 bag (300g) Quorn mince (use Quorn vegan pieces chopped up finely for a vegan alternative)
1 medium onion, finely chopped
1 clove garlic, finely chopped and crushed
3 tablespoons olive oil
2 small aubergines, washed and sliced
approximately 1 tablespoon salt to sprinkle over aubergines
14oz (400g) tin chopped tomatoes
1 teaspoon Marmite

3 tablespoons olive oil
1 tablespoon Worcester sauce (a vegetarian version of this can be bought in most health food shops)
1 tablespoon tomato puree
2 vegetable stock cubes
2 fluid oz (57mls) water
2 free range eggs
¼ pint (140mls) natural yoghurt, dairy or soya
3oz (85g) grated dairy or vegan cheddar cheese
ground sea salt and freshly ground black pepper

METHOD

1. Sprinkle salt liberally over the aubergine slices. Cover with a plate and set aside for about 20 minutes.

2. Heat 1 tablespoon olive oil in a large pan and gently fry the onion and garlic until softened.

3. Add the Quorn mince and stir into the onions.

4. Add the tin of tomatoes, Worcester sauce, Marmite, tomato puree, stock cubes, and season well with salt and pepper.

5. Pour in the 57mls of water, adding a little more if the mixture becomes too dry.

6. Simmer gently for about 5 minutes stirring well to prevent the mixture from sticking.

7. Meanwhile, rinse the aubergines well under cold running water to remove all traces of salt and pat dry with kitchen towel or a clean tea towel.

8. In a separate pan, fry the aubergine slices in the remaining 2 tablespoons olive oil until softened.
9. Place alternate layers of Quorn mixture with aubergines in a greased casserole or lasagne dish. Spread the Quorn mixture thinly to maximise taste and ensure an even spread.
10. Beat the eggs and mix in the yoghurt and grated cheddar cheese. Pour over the mince and aubergine layers.
11. Cook in a preheated oven 180°C (350°F) or Gas mark 4 for 30-40 minutes or until the top is set and golden.

Serve with either garlic bread or home made bread and a mixed salad. It could also be served with a selection of grilled or roasted vegetables.

Sausage and Cider Stew

This is a wonderful stew, full of flavour, and perfect for a cold winter day.

It is easy to make and can be made the day before, refrigerated, then reheated when required.

This recipe will make approximately 4-6 servings depending on portion size.

INGREDIENTS

½ medium butternut squash, peeled and cut into cubes
1 medium onion, chopped
1 clove garlic, crushed
1 tablespoon olive oil
1 tablespoon parsley, finely chopped
1 teaspoon dried mixed herbs

1 packet (8) Quorn sausages, defrosted and sliced
14oz (400g) tin borlotti or cannellini beans
14 fluid oz (415mls) dry cider
7 fluid oz (200mls) stock made with 2 vegetable stock cubes
1 level dessert spoon gravy powder
ground sea salt and freshly ground black pepper

METHOD

1. Gently fry the onion and garlic in the olive oil in a large pan or skillet until softened.
2. Add the butternut squash and cook for around 5 minutes until tender.
3. Add the cider, stock, sausages, parsley and mixed herbs. Bring to simmering point stirring often.
4. Open the tin of borlotti or cannellini beans, drain off the liquid and add the beans to the stew. Season well with salt and pepper.
5. Simmer gently for around 15-20 minutes.
6. Mix the gravy powder to a smooth paste with a little cold water and very gradually add to the stew, stirring to prevent lumps forming.
7. Simmer gently for a further 5 minutes, stirring well as the stew continues to thicken. Add a splash more boiling water out of the kettle if the gravy becomes too thick.

Serve with fresh seasonal vegetables and potatoes.
This stew also can be served in a bowl with a large hunk of freshly made bread for a delicious lunch.

Sausage and Leek Hotpot

This is another one of those fabulous winter warming meals. It makes your mouth water as it is taken out of the oven steaming hot, with a wonderful aroma, to be served with a plateful of fresh vegetables, potatoes and lashings of gravy. It is extremely quick and easy to make, can be made the day before, refrigerated and cooked when needed.

This recipe makes approximately 4-6 servings depending on portion size.

INGREDIENTS

1 bag (328g) or 8 Quorn sausages, defrosted
3 medium leeks, washed and sliced
2 tablespoons olive oil
14oz (400g) tin chopped tomatoes
1 heaped tablespoon dried onion
1 teaspoon dried marjoram
½ teaspoon dried basil

½ teaspoon dried oregano
1 tablespoon tomato puree
1 pint (568mls) stock made with 2 stock cubes and 1 level teaspoon Marmite
1 dessert spoon cornflour
ground sea salt and freshly ground black pepper

METHOD

1. Heat the olive oil in a large thick bottomed pan and stir in the leeks. Cover with a lid and cook over a low heat for about 10 minutes until the leeks are tender.

2. Slice the sausages and add to the pan along with the tin of tomatoes, dried onions, herbs and tomato puree.

3. Pour in the stock and mix well into the ingredients. Bring to a simmering point. Season well and transfer into an oven proof casserole dish. Cover with a lid.

4. Cook in a preheated oven at 180°C (350°F) or Gas mark 4 for 30 minutes.

5. Mix the cornflour to a smooth, runny paste with a little cold water and pour into the casserole, stirring well to prevent lumps forming as the gravy thickens.

6. Return to the oven for a further 10 minutes, stir well, adding a little extra hot water if the gravy appears too thick.

Serve immediately with potatoes, fresh seasonal vegetables and lashings of gravy.

Cheese and No Bacon Pie

This is a superb, versatile meal that can be made the day before to be cooked when needed. I make this dish in preparation for a busy day, refrigerate, and then it is ready to pop in the oven on our return. It is extremely tasty and the kids love it when they get back from a swimming lesson.

This recipe make approximately 4-6 helpings depending on portion size.

INGREDIENTS

2lb (907g) potatoes, peeled and sliced
4oz (113g) Quorn bacon slices, diced

SAUCE

1 large onion, peeled and finely chopped
2oz (56g) butter

2oz (56g) plain flour
1 pint (568ml) warmed milk
5oz (142g) grated, strong cheddar cheese for the sauce
1oz (28g) grated, strong cheddar cheese for the topping
ground sea salt and freshly ground black pepper

METHOD

1. Parboil the potato slices in boiling salted water for about 10-15 minutes until they begin to soften a little. Strain, remove from pan, and transfer to a plate on one side.
2. To make the sauce; Melt the butter in a pan, add the onion, and cook until softened. Mix in the flour and cook for about 1 minute, stirring all the time with a wooden spoon.
3. Remove from the heat and gradually stir in the milk. (I find it much quicker and easier to warm the milk prior to doing this.)
4. Return the pan to the heat and bring slowly to the boil, stirring all the time. Turn down the heat and simmer gently, still stirring until the sauce begins to thicken.
5. Stir in the Quorn bacon and 5oz (142g) grated cheese. Cook until the cheese melts, stirring continuously. Season well with the salt and pepper.
6. Add a splash of extra milk if the sauce appears too thick. Remove from heat.
7. Arrange the potatoes and sauce in layers, finishing with a layer of sauce.
8. Sprinkle with remaining grated cheese, cover with a lid and place in a preheated oven at 180°C (350°F) or Gas mark 4. Cook for approximately 45 minutes to 1 hour until the potato is soft and the bake is cooked through.
9. Remove the lid approximately 10 minutes before the end of the cooking period so that the top browns, or alternatively, finish off under the grill for a couple of minutes.

Garnish with tomatoes and chopped basil leaves.

Leek and Mushroom Casserole with Cider Sauce

This is an incredibly tasty dish that is really quick and easy to make. It is a great favourite with all the family.

This recipe will make approximately 4-6 servings depending on portion size.

INGREDIENTS

1 bag (300g) Quorn pieces
3 medium sized leeks
2oz (56g) butter
6oz (170g) mushrooms, wiped and sliced
1 teaspoon Marmite
11 fluid oz (312ml) dry cider

5 fluid oz (140mls) stock made with 2 vegetable stock cubes
1 teaspoon dried mixed herbs
ground sea salt and freshly ground black pepper
1 dessert spoon cornflour

METHOD

1. Wash the leeks well and cut into slices.
2. Melt the butter in a non-stick pan and gently cook the leeks over a low heat with a lid on for about 5-10 minutes until softened. Add the mushrooms, stirring well until cooked.
3. Mix in the Quorn pieces, herbs, dry cider, stock and Marmite. Season well and simmer gently for about 15-20 minutes.
4. Mix 1 dessert spoon cornflour with a little water and stir into the casserole. Mix well until the mixture thickens. Add a splash of boiling water if casserole appears too thick.

Serve with potatoes and seasonal vegetables.

Thyme Hot Pot with Crispy Dumplings

This is one of those recipes that is perfect for winter weather. It is a traditional dish that could have been made by your grandmother. It will give you instant warmth and sustenance when coming in from the cold.

This recipe will make approximately 4-6 generous servings depending on portion size.

INGREDIENTS

1½ bags (450g) Quorn pieces
2 tablespoons olive oil
1 large onion, chopped
1 clove garlic, crushed
6oz (170g) mushrooms, wiped with damp kitchen towel and sliced
2 tablespoons tomato puree

10 fluid oz (284mls) stock made with 1 vegetable stock cube and 1 teaspoon Marmite
1 teaspoon dried thyme
1 teaspoon Worcester sauce
ground sea salt and freshly ground black pepper
14oz (400g) tin chopped tomatoes
1 level dessert spoon gravy powder

METHOD

1. Heat the olive oil in a large frying pan and lightly fry the onion until softened, then add the garlic and mushrooms, stirring frequently.

2. Stir in the tomato puree, thyme, Quorn pieces and season well. Cook for 1 minute stirring continuously.

3. Add the tin of tomatoes, Worcester sauce and 10 fluid oz (284mls) stock to the onion, Quorn and mushroom mixture. Bring to the boil, turn the heat down and stir regularly for a couple of minutes.

4. Mix the gravy powder to a runny paste with a little water and pour into the casserole, stirring continuously as the gravy thickens, to prevent lumps forming. Add a splash of boiling water if the gravy becomes too thick.

5. Transfer into a casserole dish and place the Crispy dumplings on top of the casserole.

6. Cover with a lid and cook in a pre-heated oven 180°C (350°F) or Gas mark 4 for 40 minutes.

CRISPY DUMPLINGS

4oz (113g) butter or hard margarine, very cold and grated
8oz (226) self raising flour
ground sea salt and freshly ground black pepper
1 teaspoon dried onion

1 teaspoon dried thyme
cold water to mix (approximately 1 teaspoon per 25g of ingredients) to form a stiff dough
4oz (113g) wholemeal breadcrumbs for coating

METHOD FOR DUMPLINGS

7. Sift the flour and salt together. Add the remaining ingredients and mix together.
8. Shape into 10-15 balls and coat with breadcrumbs. Then place the dumplings on top of the casserole. *See method no. 5*

Serve with roast potatoes and seasonal vegetables.

Herby Vegetable Casserole

This is a fantastic winter dish, full of warmth and flavour. It is something that can be prepared the night before, and refrigerated until needed, which in fact improves the flavours. The mushroom ketchup is something I discovered in an old fashioned delicatessen. It is full of flavour, yet has an old fashioned quality which easily takes us back to the type of food our grandmother used to cook. This only serves to add to the comforting quality of this dish.

This casserole will make approximately 4-6 generous servings depending on portion size.

INGREDIENTS

1½ bags (450g) Quorn pieces
1 large onion, finely chopped
2 large carrots, peeled and cut into large slices
2 small sticks celery, finely chopped
1 garlic clove, crushed
2 tablespoons olive oil
1½ pints (852mls) stock made with 1½ vegetable stock cubes and 1 heaped teaspoon Marmite

1 dessert spoon Worcester sauce (a vegetarian version of this is available from most health food shops)
1 bay leaf
1 sprig fresh thyme or ½ teaspoon dried thyme
1 sprig fresh rosemary or ½ teaspoon dried rosemary
1 dessert spoon mushroom ketchup
1 tablespoon gravy powder
ground sea salt and freshly ground black pepper

METHOD

1. In a large frying pan, gently cook the onion, carrots, celery and garlic in the olive oil until they darken at the edges.

2. Transfer into a large casserole dish.

3. Add the herbs, mushroom ketchup, Worcester sauce, Marmite, stock, bay leaf and season well with salt and pepper. Mix well together.

4. Stir in the Quorn pieces, cover with a lid and cook in a preheated oven at 180°C (350°F) or Gas mark 4 for 30 minutes.

5. Remove from the oven. Mix the gravy powder into a smooth paste with a little water and stir well into the casserole mixture. Add a little more hot water if the casserole becomes too thick.

6. Return to the oven for a further 10 minutes.

Serve with roast potatoes, seasonal vegetables and gravy.

Honeyed Stew

As the name suggests, this recipe gives us a slightly sweetened version of a classic style of stew. This difference in flavours makes a refreshing change in a meal that can be enjoyed by all. It is easy to make and can easily be prepared the morning or the day before.

This recipe will make approximately 4-6 servings depending on portion size.

INGREDIENTS

1½ bags (450g) Quorn pieces
1½ pints (852mls) stock made with 1 vegetable stock cube
1 heaped teaspoon Marmite
2 tablespoons olive oil
1 large onion, peeled and chopped
3 celery stalks, washed and chopped

2 large carrots, peeled and sliced
1 tablespoon (15ml) honey
1 tablespoon (15ml) lemon juice
1 teaspoon mustard powder
1 tablespoon tomato puree
pinch chilli flakes
ground sea salt and freshly ground pepper
1 level tablespoon gravy powder

METHOD

1. Heat the oil in a large frying pan and cook the onion, celery, and carrots until soft, stirring to prevent mixture from sticking.

2. Stir in the remaining ingredients apart from the gravy powder and mix well.

3. Tip into an oven proof casserole dish and cook in a preheated oven at 180°C (350°F) or Gas mark 4 for 30 minutes.

4. Mix the gravy powder into a smooth paste with about 50mls of cold water and stir into the stew. Return to the oven for another 5-10 minutes to allow the gravy to thicken. Stir well. Add a splash of hot water if the stew becomes too thick.

Serve with green vegetables and mashed potatoes.

Cottage Pie

This is another one of those recipes that is traditional, yet remains a solid favourite for all the family. You can't go wrong with this when inviting children's friends home for tea, or for any fussy eater who is difficult to please. It is a wonderful dish for a cold winter night served with lashings of gravy. It can also be made the day before, refrigerated, and cooked when needed.

This recipe will make approximately 4-6 helpings depending on portion size and accompanying vegetables.

INGREDIENTS

2lb (907g) potatoes, peeled, washed and quartered
2 tablespoons olive oil
1 medium onion, finely chopped
2 carrots (medium to large), grated
1 bag (300g) Quorn pieces
1 heaped teaspoon Marmite
4oz (113g) frozen petit pois peas
1 tablespoon tomato puree
14oz (400g) tin chopped tomatoes
½ carton (250g) passata (sieved tomatoes)

3.5 fluid oz (100mls) vegetable stock made with 1½ vegetable stock cubes
½ teaspoon dried thyme
½ teaspoon dried rosemary
ground sea salt and freshly ground black pepper
1 dessert spoon gravy powder (mixed to a paste with 2 tablespoons cold water)
1oz (28g) butter or margarine
2 tablespoons milk
2oz (56g) grated, strong cheddar cheese to sprinkle over the top

METHOD

1. Cook the potatoes in boiling, salted water until soft. Mash with 1oz (28g) margarine or butter and 2 tablespoons milk.
2. Heat the olive oil in a large pan and cook the onions and the grated carrot until soft, stirring frequently.
3. Add the Quorn pieces, mix well into the onion and carrot mixture.
4. Mix in the tomato puree, tinned tomatoes, passata, Marmite, herbs, frozen peas and vegetable stock. Season well with salt and pepper.
5. Bring to a gentle simmer and leave to cook for about 10 minutes, stirring regularly.
6. Meanwhile, mash the potatoes with the butter and milk.
7. Mix the gravy paste into the Quorn mixture, stirring well until mixture begins to thicken, adding extra hot water if the mixture becomes too thick.
8. Pour mixture into an oven proof casserole dish and fork the mashed potato over the top.
9. Sprinkle with grated cheese.

10. Bake in a preheated oven at 180°C (350°F) or Gas mark 4 for 30-40 minutes until golden brown.

Serve with an assortment of freshly cooked vegetables and lashings of gravy.

FAMILY FAVOURITES

Cobbler

Shepherds Pie

Lamb Free Crumble

Spicy Sausage and Bean Bake

Stuffed Peppers with Quorn and Chestnuts

Chickenless Leek and Mushroom Bake
with Crunchy Topping

Stuffed Cabbage Leaves

Spaghetti Bolognese

West Downs Pie

Toad in the Hole

Savoury Crepes

Rissoles

Cobbler

This is one of those recipes from a bygone age that your grandmother used to make. The smell and the taste brings back loads of poignant memories. It is also one of those truly wonderful winter dishes that warms you from the inside out.

This will make approximately 4-6 generous servings depending on portion size.

INGREDIENTS

1½ bags (450g) Quorn pieces
1 large onion, chopped
2 medium carrots, grated
1 clove garlic, crushed
1 heaped teaspoon Marmite
1 pint (568mls) vegetable stock made with
1½ vegetable stock cubes
2 tablespoons olive oil
1 level dessert spoon gravy powder
1 teaspoon French mustard

1 teaspoon dried mixed herbs
ground sea salt and freshly ground black pepper

FOR THE TOPPING

8oz (227g) plain flour
4 teaspoons baking powder
1 level teaspoon salt
1½ oz (42g) butter
approximately ¼ pint (140mls) milk
approximately 1 tablespoon of plain flour to coat hands and flour the worktop

METHOD

1. Heat the oil in a large frying pan and gently cook the onions, carrots and garlic, stirring regularly, until softened.

2. Stir in the stock, Marmite, mustard, herbs and Quorn pieces. Season well.

3. Bring to the boil mixing all the time. Turn down the heat and simmer gently for about 10 minutes, stirring regularly.

4. Turn into a 3 pint casserole dish and cook in a preheated oven 180°C (350°F) or Gas mark 4 for 30 minutes.

TO MAKE THE TOPPING

5. Sift the flour, baking powder and salt into a bowl, then rub in the butter until the mixture resembles fine breadcrumbs.

6. Add the milk gradually to give a soft, but not sticky dough.

7. Lightly coat hands with flour to prevent the dough from sticking and knead lightly until smooth.

8. Roll out on a floured surface to 1cm (½ inch) thickness. Then cut out rounds with a 5cm (2 inch) cutter. Makes about 10 rounds.

METHOD

9. Remove the casserole from the oven at the end of the 30 minutes cooking time.

10. Mix 1 dessert spoon of gravy powder with a little cold water to make a smooth paste. Add this to the casserole and stir well as the casserole thickens. Add a splash more hot water if the mixture becomes too thick.

11. Arrange the topping rounds on top of the casserole and brush with milk.

12. Increase the heat to moderately hot, 190°C (375°)F or Gas mark 5. Bake for about 15 minutes until the Cobbler is golden brown.

Serve with mashed potatoes, plenty of
seasonal vegetables and lashings of gravy.

Shepherds Pie

This is my version of this traditional dish. A guaranteed favourite of all, young and old alike. I can give this to my children's friends or to grandparents, knowing that it will be thoroughly enjoyed and the plate emptied. I can fool most meat eaters into thinking this is the real thing, but they don't really care once they taste it, as it tastes so good.

This will make approximately 4-5 portions depending on portion size.

INGREDIENTS

½ bag (150g) Quorn mince
2 tablespoons olive oil
1 medium onion, chopped
2 medium carrots, grated
½ carton (250g) passata (sieved tomatoes)
1 tablespoon tomato puree
½ pint (284mls) hot water with one vegetable stock cube dissolved in it
1 heaped teaspoon Marmite

¼ teaspoon dried thyme
¼ teaspoon dried rosemary
1 dessert spoon gravy powder
1¾ lb (794g) potatoes, peeled, washed and quartered
1oz (28g) butter or margarine
2 tablespoons milk
2oz (56g) strong cheddar cheese, grated
ground sea salt and freshly ground black pepper

METHOD

1. Cook the potatoes in boiling salted water for about 20-25 minutes until soft.
2. While the potatoes are boiling, in a large frying pan, gently fry the onions and the grated carrot in the olive oil until soft.
3. Add the Quorn mince, tomato puree, passata, vegetable stock, Marmite and herbs. Season well with salt and pepper.
4. Bring to simmering point and simmer gently for about 5-10 minutes.
5. Mix the gravy powder to a smooth paste with a little cold water and add to mixture, stirring well as the mixture begins to thicken.
6. Pour into a 1 litre (2 pint) oven proof dish.
7. Mash the potato with butter or margarine and 2 tablespoons milk and use to top the Quorn mixture.
8. Use the prongs of a fork to decorate the potato and sprinkle grated cheese over the top.
9. Bake in a preheated oven at 180°C (350°F) or Gas mark 4 for about 30-40 minutes until golden brown on top.

Serve with seasonal fresh vegetables and gravy.

Lamb Free Crumble

I have tried to create a lamb flavour in this dish, which I think does work. It is delicious served as a Sunday dinner with roast potatoes, lots of vegetables and gravy.

This recipe will make 4-6 helpings depending on portion size and accompanying vegetables.

INGREDIENTS

1 bag (300g) Quorn mince
1 medium onion, finely chopped
2 tablespoons olive oil
1 dessert spoon gravy powder
1 teaspoon Marmite
½ pint (284mls) vegetable stock made with one vegetable stock cube

dried thyme, basil and rosemary, pinch of each
1 tablespoon mint jelly
ground sea salt and freshly ground black pepper

INGREDIENTS FOR CRUMBLE TOPPING

4oz (113g) plain flour
2oz (56g) butter
2oz (56g) mature cheddar cheese, grated

METHOD

1. In a large frying pan, heat the oil and fry the onion until soft. Add the Quorn mince and cook, mixing well until thoroughly defrosted.

2. Add the tomato puree, vegetable stock, Marmite and dried herbs. Bring gently to a simmer, and cook over a low heat stirring well for 5-10 minutes.

3. Mix the gravy powder with a little water into a smooth paste, and pour into the Quorn mixture, stirring well to prevent lumps forming as the gravy begins to thicken.

4. Finally, add the mint jelly. Turn the heat down to low and simmer gently for 5-10 minutes while making the crumble mix. Stir well to ensure the mix doesn't burn. Add a splash of hot water if mixture becomes too thick.

METHOD FOR CRUMBLE TOPPING

5. In a bowl, rub the butter into the flour until it resembles fine breadcrumbs. Stir in the grated cheese and season with salt and pepper.

6. Tip the Quorn mixture into a shallow oven proof dish and spoon the crumble mixture over the Quorn base.

7. Bake in the oven at 180°C (350°F) or Gas mark 4 for about 30-40 minutes until golden brown.

Serve immediately with roast potatoes, seasonal vegetables and lashings of gravy.

Spicy Sausage and Bean Bake

The title says it all, but it doesn't describe the full flavour of this dish, along with the satisfying feeling of fullness due to the high protein content.

This can be served with roasted potatoes and vegetables as shown in the photograph, or with rice or enchiladas to give a real Mexican feel.

On a more simplistic note, serve with freshly made bread for a wholesome and hearty lunch.

This will serve 4-6 depending on portion size.

INGREDIENTS

8 Quorn frozen sausages, defrosted and cut into slices
2 sticks celery, washed and chopped
1 large onion finely, chopped
1 large clove garlic, crushed
1 red and 1 green pepper, washed, deseeded and chopped
1 red chilli, washed and finely chopped
2 tablespoons olive oil
14oz (400g) tin mixed beans, drained

14oz (400g) tin chopped tomatoes
7oz (198g) frozen sweetcorn
1 glass of red wine
1 teaspoon dried mixed herbs
5 fluid oz (140 mls) stock made with 2 vegetable stock cubes
2 tablespoons tomato puree
1 teaspoon mushroom ketchup
ground sea salt and freshly ground black pepper
2 tablespoons chopped herbs to garnish

METHOD

1. Heat the oil in a large thick bottomed pan and add the chopped onions and celery, mixing well until they begin to soften.

2. Add the crushed garlic, chopped peppers and chilli, mix well and continue to fry until cooked.

3. Mix in the remaining ingredients, bring to the boil, turn down the heat and allow to simmer gently for about 15-20 minutes until all the ingredients have cooked in together and the liquid has reduced to a gravy like consistency.

4. Add a splash of boiling water if mixture becomes too thick.

To serve, season well and garnish with chopped herbs.

Stuffed Peppers with Quorn and Chestnuts

This is a recipe that will always impress your guests. The cooked pepper works incredibly well to compliment the combined tastes of the Quorn and the chestnut puree. The colourful red peppers look fantastic and will set off any dinner party or buffet.

This recipe will make 4 portions.

INGREDIENTS

½ bag (150g) Quorn mince
8oz (227g) chestnut puree (tinned)
4 large red peppers
1 medium onion, chopped
4oz (113g) mushrooms, washed and chopped
2 tablespoons olive oil

1 teaspoon Marmite
4 fluid oz (114mls) stock made with 2 vegetable stock cubes
1 teaspoon Worcester sauce (a vegetarian version can be found in most Health Food shops)
ground sea salt and freshly ground black pepper

METHOD

1. Cut the tops off the peppers, de-seed and simmer the tops and the body of each pepper in slightly salted water for 5 minutes. Remove from pan and drain well.

2. In a large pan or skillet, gently fry the onion and mushrooms in the olive oil until softened, stirring regularly.

3. Add the Quorn mince and cook until defrosted.

4. Mix in the stock, Marmite, Worcester sauce, salt and pepper, stirring well until all the ingredients have been thoroughly blended together and begin to simmer.

5. Cook, stirring well for about 5-10 minutes.

6. Add the chestnut puree and mix together. Season well with salt and pepper.

7. Place the peppers in an oven proof dish and stuff with the Quorn and chestnut mixture, pressing down well into each pepper. Place the tops back on the peppers.

8. Cook in a preheated oven at 180°C (350°F) or Gas mark 4 for about 20- 30 minutes.

Serve with salad and new potatoes, or mashed potatoes and grilled tomatoes.

Chickenless Leek and Mushroom Bake with Crunchy Topping

This is a dish that is rich in flavour, colour and texture. It can be served for many different occasions and can be made the day before and cooked as needed. It is also deceptively easy to make. I usually prefer to use olive oil, rather than butter in my recipes. However, butter seems to work much better in this recipe, as it gives an extra richness to the flavour, which is maybe needed when cooking with leeks.

This dish makes approximately 4-6 helpings depending on portion size.

INGREDIENTS

1lb (454g) leeks, washed and sliced
8oz (227g) mushrooms, washed and sliced
1 clove garlic, crushed
1 bag (300g) Quorn pieces
2oz (56g) butter or margarine
1 small glass of white wine
2 vegetable stock cubes

¼ pint (140mls) hot water
1 level tablespoon cornflour
2 fluid oz (57mls) milk
4oz (113g) mature cheddar cheese, grated
1 crust of bread made into breadcrumbs
(100g approximately)
1 tablespoon olive oil
ground sea salt and freshly ground black pepper

METHOD

1. Sweat the leeks in the butter in a pan with a lid for about 10 minutes until tender.

2. Add the mushrooms and garlic and continue to cook over a low heat until soft. Mix in the Quorn pieces and cook until thoroughly defrosted.

3. Add the wine and simmer for a couple of minutes to allow the flavours to mix.

4. Dissolve the stock cubes in the ¼ pint (140mls) hot water and add to Quorn mixture stirring well while bringing back to simmering point.

5. Season well with salt and pepper.

6. Mix the cornflour to a runny paste with the 2 fluid oz (57mls) milk. Blend this into the Quorn mixture.

7. Stir well as the mixture begins to thicken. Add a splash more milk if the consistency becomes too thick.

8. Transfer into an oven proof casserole dish.

9. Mix the breadcrumbs and grated cheese together with 1 tablespoon of olive oil. Mix well, then sprinkle over the top of the bake.

10. Bake in a preheated oven at 180°C (350°F) or Gas mark 4 for about 30 minutes until the topping is golden brown.

Serve with a baked potato and salad, or with new potatoes and a selection of vegetables.

Stuffed Cabbage Leaves

This is my version of this traditional Greek dish. It is tasty and original in its texture and appearance.

This dish makes 4-6 helpings depending on portion size.

INGREDIENTS

1 medium firm cabbage
1 bag (300g) Quorn mince
1 medium onion, finely chopped
2 tablespoons olive oil
4 tablespoons porridge oats

2 teaspoons Worcester sauce
14 fluid oz (415mls) stock from cabbage leaf cooking water with 2 vegetable stock cubes and 1 teaspoon Marmite
ground sea salt and freshly ground black pepper

METHOD

1. Prepare the cabbage leaves by pulling or cutting approximately 8 from the base of the cabbage. Wash in cold water and remove part of the thick centre ridge if it appears tough.

2. Place the leaves in a large pan, cover with boiling water and cook for about 10 minutes until the the leaves begin to soften.

3. Drain and retain the water to make the 14 fluid oz (398mls) stock with the stock cubes and Marmite. Cool the leaves in a basin of cold water.

4. Heat the olive oil in a frying pan and cook the onion gently over a low heat until softened. Add the Quorn, 4 fluid oz (114mls) of the Marmite stock and continue to cook for a few more minutes, stirring well.

5. Add seasoning, oats, and Worcester sauce. (A vegetarian version of this can be bought in most health food shops). Mix together well and remove from heat.

6. Drain the cabbage, and lie each leaf flat on the table. Place about a tablespoon of Quorn mixture in the centre of each cabbage leaf, until the mixture is equally divided between all the leaves.

7. Make a parcel of the Quorn mixture and place in an oven proof dish. Pour over the remaining stock, cover and cook in a pre-heated oven at 180°C (350°F) or Gas mark 4 for 30 minutes. Do not allow the leaf parcels to over brown.

Serve with roast potatoes, seasonal vegetables and gravy.

Spaghetti Bolognese

This is my version of the classic favourite. It is loved by all and the basic bolognese mixture can be used to make lasagne and other Italian dishes.

This recipe generously makes 4-6 portions.

INGREDIENTS

2 tablespoons olive oil
1 large onion, finely chopped
1 red pepper, finely chopped
6oz (170g) mushrooms, wiped and chopped
1 bag (300g) Quorn mince
500g carton passata (sieved tomatoes)
1 large or 2 small cloves garlic, crushed
1 level teaspoon dried basil
1 level teaspoon dried marjoram

1 level teaspoon dried oregano
1 heaped tablespoon tomato puree
1½ vegetable stock cubes
1 heaped teaspoon Marmite
ground sea salt and freshly ground black pepper
1 level dessert spoon gravy powder
1 small glass red wine
4 fluid oz (114mls) hot water
parmesan cheese to serve
basil leaves to garnish

METHOD

1. Gently fry the chopped onion, garlic and pepper in the olive oil until softened. Add the mushrooms and continue to fry until cooked.

2. Add the Quorn mince and stir well until defrosted and mixed in with the vegetables.

3. Add the passata, stirring well. Mix in the tomato puree, herbs, stock cubes, red wine and season well with salt and pepper. Stir in the teaspoon of Marmite.

4. Add 4 fluid oz (114mls) hot water. Bring to simmering point and allow to simmer gently for about 15 minutes, stirring regularly.

5. Mix the gravy powder to a smooth paste with a little cold water and stir well into the bolognese mixture, stirring continually until the mixture thickens. Add a splash more hot water if the bolognese appears too thick.

Serve on a bed of spaghetti with parmesan cheese grated over the top and garnish with chopped basil leaves.

West Downs Pie

This is a delicious variation to my Shepherds Pie recipe. With its rich onion and red wine gravy, this provides a very tasty change to the old favourite.

INGREDIENTS

½ bag (150g) Quorn mince
2 tablespoons olive oil
1 medium onion, finely chopped
1 clove garlic, crushed
1 medium carrot, grated
1 teaspoon dried mixed herbs
6oz (170g) passata (sieved tomatoes)
1 small glass red wine
1 tablespoon tomato puree

5 fluid oz (140mls) stock made with 1½ vegetable stock cubes
1 level teaspoon Marmite
1 level dessert spoon gravy powder
ground sea salt and freshly ground black pepper
1½lb (680g) potatoes, peeled and quartered
1oz (28g) butter
1 tablespoon milk
2oz (56g) grated, strong cheddar cheese for topping

METHOD

1. Peel and cook the potatoes in boiling, salted water for about 25-30 minutes.
2. Heat the oil in a large pan and cook the onion and garlic until beginning to soften. Add the grated carrot, and continue to cook stirring regularly for a couple of minutes.
3. Add the red wine and simmer gently for a few minutes to reduce the wine and enhance the flavour.
4. Add the Quorn mince and stir well into the red wine gravy. Add the stock, Marmite, passata, herbs and season well with salt and pepper.
5. Allow to simmer over a low heat, stirring regularly, for about 5-10 minutes. Add a little more water if mixture becomes too dry.
6. Mix the gravy powder with a little cold water to make a runny paste and pour, while mixing well into the Quorn mixture. Add splash of hot water if gravy thickens too much. Tip into an oven proof casserole dish. Spread evenly across the base of the dish.
7. Once the potatoes are soft, drain and mash with the butter and milk to a smooth consistency, then arrange on top of the mince. Using the prongs of a fork, make decorative patterns on the mashed potato and sprinkle the grated cheese over the top.
8. Cook in a preheated oven at 180°C (350°F) or Gas mark 4 for 30–40 minutes until golden brown.

Serve with fresh vegetables and lashings of gravy.

Toad in the Hole

This is one of those dishes that your grandmother used to make on a cold winters day. Just the look and smell of it will bring back comforting memories of a bygone era. Most children and adults will eat this and ask for seconds.

This recipe will make 4-6 helpings depending on portion size and accompanying vegetables.

INGREDIENTS

8 Quorn sausages (defrosted)

YORKSHIRE PUDDING BATTER

6oz (170g) plain flour

¾ pint (424mls) milk
2 eggs (beaten)
2oz (56g) butter or margarine
pinch salt

METHOD

1. Arrange the sausages neatly in the bottom of a suitable roasting tray or shallow earthenware dish.
2. Make the Yorkshire Pudding batter by sieving the flour and salt into a basin.
3. Make a well in the centre and add the egg and half the milk. Whisk to a smooth mixture.
4. Gradually add the rest of the milk, whisk well and pour over the sausages.
5. Cook in a hot oven 220° (425°F) or Gas mark 7 for approximately 30 minutes until the batter is golden brown..

Serve with roast, mashed or new potatoes, seasonal vegetables and a generous helping of gravy.

Savoury Crepes

This is one of my favourite recipes. It looks and tastes delicious, and can be served for most occasions.

This recipe will make approximately 8 filled Crepes.

INGREDIENTS FOR FILLING

1 bag (300g) Quorn mince
2 tablespoons olive oil
1 medium onion, chopped
1 clove garlic, crushed
4 oz (113g) mushrooms, wiped and chopped
7oz (200g) small tin baked beans
7oz (200g) small tin chopped tomatoes
1 tablespoon tomato puree
½ teaspoon dried basil
4 fluid oz (114mls) stock made with 1½
vegetable stock cubes
1 heaped teaspoon Marmite
1 dessert spoon gravy powder
small glass red wine
sea salt and ½ teaspoon cayenne pepper

INGREDIENTS FOR CREPES

8oz (227g) plain flour
1 teaspoon baking powder
pinch salt
2 eggs
1 pint (568ml) milk

INGREDIENTS FOR CHEESE SAUCE

1oz (28g) butter
1oz (28g) plain flour
1 pint (568ml) milk, warmed in a pan or microwave
4oz (113g) strong cheese, grated.
1oz (28g) cheese, grated for the topping.
oil for frying

METHOD FOR FILLING

1. Heat the oil in a large pan, and gently fry the onion until soft. Add the mushrooms, stirring regularly until cooked.

2. Mix in the Quorn mince, until defrosted.

3. Add the beans, tomatoes, tomato puree, Marmite, basil and stock. Season to taste with salt and cayenne pepper. Cook, stirring well for about 10-15 minutes.

4. Blend the gravy powder with a little water and add to the Quorn mixture, stirring all the time as the mixture thickens.

5. Stir in the wine and simmer gently while the crepes are being prepared. Add a splash of extra hot water if the mixture becomes too dry.

METHOD FOR CREPES

6. Sift the flour, salt and baking powder into a bowl. Beat in the egg and blend in the milk gradually.

7. Whisk the batter until smooth.

8. Oil a frying pan and heat until a faint blue haze arises. Pour in 3 tablespoons of batter, tilting the pan so that it spreads evenly.

9. Cook until golden, then turn the crepe over to cook the other side. Turn out onto a plate and repeat method numbers 8 and 9 until all the crepe mixture has been used up.

10. Place a good tablespoon of filling in the middle of each crepe and roll up.

METHOD FOR CHEESE SAUCE

11. Melt the butter in a thick bottomed pan over a low heat. Remove the pan from the heat and blend in the flour, stirring well with a wooden spoon. Return the pan to the heat for a couple of minutes stirring continuously.

12. Remove from heat and stir in some of the milk, a little at a time while mixing well. Gradually add the milk and return the pan to the heat stirring all the time.

13. The sauce will begin to thicken as it heats through. Continue stirring to prevent lumps forming. You want a consistency similar to pouring custard.

14. Add the 4oz (113g) cheese to the sauce and keep stirring until the cheese has melted.

15. Place the filled and rolled crepes onto a flat baking dish, pour the cheese sauce over the top, sprinkle with grated cheese and brown quickly under the grill.

Serve with a fresh green salad or a mixture
of cooked vegetables.

Rissoles

I remember my Gran making these with the left over meat from the joint. They are a recipe from post war Britain when there was no food wastage and every scrap was used. This is my version without the meat. My family thinks they taste great. I hope you do too.

This recipe will make around 8 Rissoles depending on size.

INGREDIENTS

½ packet (150g) Quorn mince
3 fluid oz (85ml) hot water with 1 teaspoon
Marmite dissolved in it
1½ vegetable stock cubes
½ teaspoon dried mixed herbs
3oz (85g) fresh breadcrumbs (brown)

1 small onion or 2 shallots, chopped
1 small garlic clove, crushed
1 egg
ground sea salt and freshly ground black pepper
plain flour for shaping
olive oil for frying

METHOD

1. In a saucepan, mix the hot water and Marmite, mixed herbs and stock cube with the Quorn mince.

2. Heat gently, stirring well, until the ingredients are well mixed together and the mixture has reached simmering point.

3. Blend the onion or shallots and garlic in a food processor or blender until a puree like consistency is formed.

4. Add the Quorn mixture from the pan and continue to blend until smooth.

5. In a large bowl, mix the Quorn and onion mixture with the breadcrumbs and the egg.

6. Season well.

7. Coat your hands well with the flour and take a small handful of the mixture and place on a floured worktop.

8. Shape into a round burger type shape about 2cm deep. Aim to make about 8 rissoles.

9. Heat about 3 tablespoons olive oil in a large frying pan and gently cook each rissole on both sides until golden brown.

10. Alternatively, they can be used as a burger in a bap, or with freshly made bread and a green salad.

Serve with traditional vegetables, mashed potatoes
and lashings of gravy.

SPECIAL OCCASIONS

Nut Roast

Coq Au Vin

Nut Wellington

Fillets with Cranberries and Red Wine

Gougere with Mediterranean Style Vegetables

Spiced Meat Free Balls with Chilli Sauce

Yuletide No Meat Balls

Moussaka

Tagine

Nut Roast

This is a meal for every occasion and perhaps the most versatile recipe in this book. Its taste and texture lends itself to salads, cold tables and hot meals alike. Serve with a selection of cooked vegetables and gravy for an alternative to a roast dinner. Alternatively, this roast is delicious sliced between hunks of fresh bread for a fantastic sandwich. Add stuffing for that extra seasonal flavour.

The Nut Roast can be carved into 8-10 slices depending on thickness.

INGREDIENTS

1 bag (300g) Quorn mince
1 large onion, chopped
2 large carrots, grated
2 tablespoons olive oil
8oz (227g) cashew nuts, ground

1 teaspoon Marmite
4 fluid oz (114mls) stock made with 1 vegetable stock cube
1 teaspoon dried mixed herbs
1 free range egg
ground sea salt and freshly ground black pepper

METHOD

1. In a large pan or skillet, heat the olive oil and gently fry the chopped onion and grated carrots until soft, stirring regularly.
2. Add the Quorn mince and stir well to incorporate all the ingredients.
3. Add the stock, Marmite, mixed herbs and mix well. Allow the mixture to simmer gently for a few minutes. Season well with salt and pepper. Mix in the ground cashew nuts. Take off the heat.
4. Beat the egg and stir well into the mixture.
5. Place in a greased, lined, loaf tin, and press down well with a fork. Cover with foil, and bake in a preheated oven 180°C (350°F) or Gas mark 4 for 50 minutes.
6. Remove the foil and bake for a further 10 minutes to brown the top.
7. Turn out onto a plate or tray, cut into slices and serve as a roast dinner, in a sandwich, with a tray of roasted vegetables or any other way you like.

This nut roast makes a really special alternative to turkey on Christmas Day. Serve with stuffing and a port and cranberry gravy and you will never miss turkey again.

Coq Au Vin

This is my version of this famous French dish which roughly translated means 'Chicken in Wine.

Obviously, for the purposes of this book, the 'Coq' or 'Chicken' has been replaced with Quorn.

This recipe will make approximately 4-6 helpings depending on portion size.

INGREDIENTS

1 large bag (500g) Quorn pieces or Quorn chicken fillets
Note. If using fillets, defrost before use.

1 medium onion, finely chopped
6 shallots, peeled and cut into halves or quarters
2 cloves garlic, peeled and crushed
10oz (284g) field or baby button mushrooms, wiped with pieces of damp kitchen towel

1oz (28g) butter
3 tablespoons of balsamic vinegar
5 fluid ounces (140mls) red wine
1 pint (568mls) vegetable stock made with 2 vegetable stock cubes
2 fresh thyme sprigs or 1 heaped teaspoon of dried thyme
2 tablespoons of tomato puree
2 bay leaves
ground sea salt and freshly ground black pepper

METHOD

1. Heat the butter in a large frying pan or skillet. Add the onions, shallots, garlic and cook, stirring well, until the onions and shallots have softened.

2. Add the mushrooms and stir well into the onion mixture. Cook for a couple of minutes.

3. Pour in the balsamic vinegar and bring to the boil until it has reduced by half. Add the red wine, and bring to a simmering point. Season well.

4. Mix in the Quorn pieces or Quorn chicken fillets.

5. Incorporate the remaining ingredients and bring back to to the boil. Turn down the heat and simmer gently for about 5 minutes. Add a splash of boiling water if the mixture becomes too dry.

6. Transfer the Coq Au Vin into an oven proof casserole dish and place in a preheated oven at 180°C (350°F) or Gas mark 4 for 30 minutes.

Serve with roast potatoes and fresh seasonal vegetables.

Nut Wellington

This is my version of this delicious dish that looks and tastes fantastic, and never fails to impress the guests.

INGREDIENTS

1 425g pack ready rolled puff pastry
1 medium onion, finely chopped
2 tablespoons olive oil
6oz (170g) button mushrooms, wiped with damp kitchen towel and coarsely chopped
6oz (170g) mixed nuts
3oz (85g) breadcrumbs
½ bag (150g) Quorn mince
1 teaspoon dried rosemary
1 clove garlic, crushed

juice of ½ lemon
1 dessert spoon mushroom ketchup (this can be found in most major supermarkets and delicatessens)
1 tablespoon finely chopped parsley
sea salt and freshly ground black pepper
1 beaten egg
2 tablespoons vegetable stock made with ½ vegetable stock cube and ½ teaspoon Marmite
2 tablespoons milk to glaze the plait

METHOD

1. Heat the oil in a pan and gently cook the onion and garlic until softened. Add the mushrooms and cook, stirring well.

2. Add the Quorn mince, stock, herbs, lemon juice and mushroom ketchup. Cook, stirring well for about 5 minutes to allow the flavours to infuse.

3. Finely chop the nuts in a blender or food processor until smooth. Stir into the Quorn mixture.

4. Remove from heat. Add the breadcrumbs, beaten egg and season well with salt and pepper.

5. Roll the pastry into a rectangle and place on a greased and floured baking tray. Spoon the mixture down the middle leaving enough pastry at either end to cover the ends of the plait.

6. On either side of filling, cut the pastry into diagonal strips about 2cm wide. Fold these over the filling to make a plait pattern over the top and tuck in the ends.

7. Brush with milk and cook in a pre-heated oven 190°C (375°F) or Gas mark 5 for 30-40 minutes until golden brown.

Serve with a salad or as a roast dinner with roast potatoes, vegetables and red currant jelly

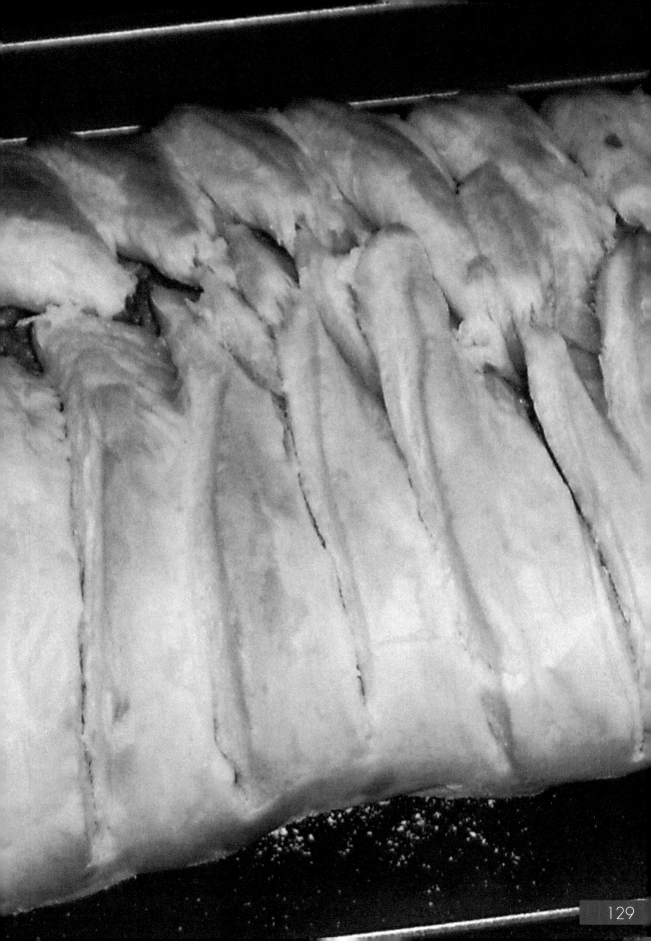

Fillets with Cranberries and Red Wine

This is a dish that is something a little different, tastes fantastic, and really gets the taste buds going.

It is very easy to make and can be used for a delicious family meal, but would really wow the guests for a dinner party.

This recipe will make approximately 4-6 helpings depending on portion size.

INGREDIENTS

312g packet, 6 Quorn chicken fillets (defrosted but not cooked)
2 tablespoons olive oil
6-8 shallots, roughly chopped
1 clove garlic, crushed
2 tablespoons cranberry sauce
300g tin tomato soup

¼ pint (142mls) red wine
4 fluid oz (114mls) stock made with 1 teaspoon Marmite and 1½ stock cubes
Juice of ½ lemon
7oz (198g) button mushrooms, wiped with damp kitchen towel and sliced
ground sea salt and freshly ground black pepper

METHOD

1. Gently cook the shallots and garlic in the olive oil until soft.
2. Add the mushrooms and cook stirring regularly.
3. Pour in the red wine, turn up the heat and simmer until the wine has reduced in quantity by half.
4. Add the cranberry sauce, soup, stock and lemon juice. Season well.
5. Simmer over a low heat for about 5 minutes, stirring regularly to incorporate the flavours.
6. Put the Quorn fillets into an oven proof casserole dish and pour the sauce mixture over the top. Cook in a preheated oven at 180°C (350°F) or Gas mark 4 for 30-40 minutes.

Serve with fresh seasonal vegetables, mashed, roast or new potatoes.

131

Gougere with Mediterranean Style Vegetables

This recipe is really one to wow the guests. The Choux pastry surround conjures up cordon bleu recipes and looks far more complicated and elaborate than it actually is, but don't tell anyone!

It tastes wonderful and really does melt in your mouth. Choux pastry is actually very easy to make, and if you follow this recipe carefully, you will also be able to create a meal to rival the chefs.

This recipe will make approximately 4-6 portions depending on portion size and accompaniments.

Choux Pastry

9 fluid oz (250mls) water
4oz (113g) butter
5oz (142g) plain flour
4 eggs
4oz (112g) grated cheddar cheese
ground sea salt and freshly ground black pepper

Filling

2oz (56g) chopped Quorn bacon
1oz (28g) butter
1 medium onion, chopped
1 clove garlic, crushed

2 red peppers, deseeded and quartered
1 tablespoon olive oil
1 small glass (120mls) red wine
1oz (28g) plain flour
¼ pint (140mls) stock, made with 2 vegetable stock cubes
14oz (400g) vine tomatoes, peeled and chopped
pinch of dried mixed herbs
ground black pepper and freshly ground sea salt
1 tablespoon parmesan cheese, grated
1 tablespoon chopped basil leaves

Method for Choux pastry

1. Sift the flour onto a plate.
2. Put the water and butter in a large saucepan. Bring to the boil, ensuring the butter has melted. Remove from the heat and, whilst still bubbling, tip in all the flour.
3. Stir vigorously until smooth (a couple of minutes).
4. Cool mixture for about 5 minutes, then beat in the eggs, one at a time. Beat for about 3 minutes until glossy.
5. Stir in the cheese and season to taste with salt and pepper.
6. Grease a pie plate or oven proof dish and arrange the choux pastry around the sides. Leave a hollow in the centre.

METHOD FOR FILLING

7. Place the red peppers on a baking tray, drizzle with olive oil and place in a preheated oven at 220°C (425°F) or Gas Mark 7. Cook for 15 minutes on one side then turn over, drizzle with more olive oil and cook for 15 minutes on the other side. Chop into small pieces.

8. Melt the butter in a saucepan and gently fry the onion and garlic until soft. Add the chopped red pepper.

9. Pour in the red wine, turn up the heat and allow the mixture to boil until the red wine has at least halved in volume. Season well with salt and pepper.

10. Remove from heat and blend in the flour followed by the stock. Return to the heat and stir continuously until the mixture thickens.

11. Remove from the heat and add the Quorn bacon, tomato and mixed herbs. Pour the filling into the centre of the Choux pastry and sprinkle the top with parmesan cheese.

12. Bake in pre-heated oven 200°C (400°F) or Gas mark 6 for 30-40 minutes until golden brown and well risen.

Sprinkle with chopped basil leaves and serve immediately.

133

Spiced Meat Free Balls with Chilli Sauce

This is a spicy and very tasty dish. The sauce is extremely easy to make and can be made beforehand, and even frozen if necessary. The meat free balls will keep well in the fridge overnight, ready to be cooked the next day.

This recipe will make approximately 4-6 helpings depending on portion sizes.

Serve with plain boiled rice.

MEAT FREE BALLS

1 bag (300g) Quorn mince
1 medium onion, chopped
1 clove of garlic crushed
1 tablespoon olive oil
pinch dried thyme, basil and rosemary
1 teaspoon each of cumin and coriander
1oz (28g) pecan nuts
3½ fluid oz (100mls) stock made with 1
vegetable stock cube and 1 teaspoon Marmite
1 egg, beaten
ground sea salt and freshly ground black
pepper

1oz (28g) plain flour

CHILLI SAUCE

1 red chilli, de-seeded and chopped
1 medium onion, finely chopped
2 cloves garlic, crushed
1 tablespoon of olive oil
1 tablespoon of balsamic vinegar
500g carton passata (sieved tomatoes)
1 heaped teaspoon sugar
3½ fluid oz (100mls) hot water
1 vegetable stock cube
sea salt and freshly ground black pepper
chopped parsley to garnish

METHOD FOR THE MEAT FREE BALLS

1. Put the Quorn mince and 100mls stock in a pan over a low heat and cook the mince until it has defrosted and absorbed the stock.

2. Add the dried herbs, cumin, coriander, salt and pepper. Continue to cook for another couple of minutes, stirring regularly, then remove from heat.

3. In a large frying pan or skillet, gently fry the chopped onion and garlic in the olive oil until soft.

4. Transfer into a food processor or blender and add the Quorn mixture, egg and ground pecan nuts. Blend for a few minutes until smooth.

5. Remove the mixture from the food processor and using the flour to coat your hands, mould into balls about the size of walnuts. You should have around 12-15 balls.

6. Place these on a greased baking tray and bake in a preheated oven at 200°C (400°F) or Gas mark 6. Cook for 15-20mins, turning halfway through the cooking time, until the balls are golden brown.

7. While the balls are cooking, cook your rice and make your chilli sauce.

METHOD FOR THE CHILLI SAUCE

8. Heat the oil in a non stick pan and gently cook the onion, chilli and garlic, stirring regularly until soft. Add the balsamic vinegar, mix in well and cook for a couple of minutes until the vinegar has reduced by half in volume.

9. Add the passata. Use the 100mls hot water to rinse out the passata carton to get every bit of taste into the meal and pour into the mixture.

10. Add the sugar, stock cube, salt and pepper. Simmer gently for a couple of minutes, stirring regularly.

Serve on a bed of rice, pour the chilli sauce over the top and garnish with chopped parsley.

135

Yuletide No Meat Balls

Meat Balls are one of Sweden's favourite dishes. There is a different recipe for every occasion. This is my Christmas version, I hope you enjoy it.

Recipe makes approximately 4-6 helpings depending on portion size.

INGREDIENTS

1 medium onion, peeled and finely chopped
2 cloves garlic, crushed
1 large bag (500g) Quorn mince
3-4 tablespoons of olive oil
1 teaspoon Marmite
4 fluid oz (114mls) stock made with 2 vegetable stock cubes
3oz (85g) fresh brown breadcrumbs
1 tablespoon tomato puree
1 teaspoon ground cumin
1 teaspoon ground coriander
1 teaspoon ground paprika
2 medium eggs, beaten
freshly ground sea salt and freshly ground black pepper

1 tablespoon of plain flour to coat hands.

SAUCE

1oz (28g) each of roughly chopped onion, carrot and celery
1oz (28g) butter or margarine
1 tablespoon malt vinegar
sprig of thyme
½ pint (284mls) boiling water with 1 stock cube dissolved in it
ground sea salt and freshly ground black pepper
grated rind and juice of 1 orange
1 x 250ml jar of cranberry sauce
1 tablespoon of port wine
a few peppercorns
coarsely grated orange rind to garnish

METHOD FOR NO MEAT BALLS

1. Heat 1 tablespoon oil in a large thick bottomed frying pan, then add the onions and garlic, stirring regularly until soft and beginning to brown at the edges.

2. Mix in the Quorn mince with the 4 fluid oz (114mls) of vegetable stock and Marmite.

3. Stir in the cumin, coriander, paprika, tomato puree, season well with salt and pepper.

4. Simmer for about 5 minutes to incorporate the flavours and reduce any liquid that is left then take off the heat, and allow the contents to cool for about 15 minutes.

5. Mix in the eggs and then blend the mixture in a food processor or blender until smooth. Stir in the breadcrumbs.

6. Coat hands with flour. Take 1 heaped dessert spoon of the mixture and roll into an even sized ball. Set aside on a plate and repeat until all the mixture has been formed into balls.

7. Heat the remaining oil in a large thick bottomed frying pan. Gently place the No Meat Balls in the pan, reduce the heat and turn regularly until evenly browned all over.

8. Remove from the pan and drain off any excess oil. Turn into an oven proof serving dish. Place in a preheated oven at 120°C (248°F) or Gas mark 1 to retain the heat while the sauce is made.

METHOD FOR SAUCE

9. Fry the onion, carrot and celery in the butter or margarine until softened.

10. Add the thyme, peppercorns and vinegar, continue to cook for a couple of minutes stirring regularly until the vinegar has halved in volume.

11. Pour in the stock and simmer gently for 5 minutes. Strain through a sieve to remove the onion, carrot, celery and peppercorns. Be careful to retain the liquid for the sauce. Transfer the liquid to a clean pan.

12. Add the port wine, cranberry sauce and grated rind and juice of the orange. Season well with salt and pepper.

13. Take the No Meat Balls out of the oven and pour the sauce mix over the top.

Garnish with orange rind and herbs and serve with roast potatoes, vegetables and lashings of gravy.

137

Moussaka

This is my version of this well known Greek dish. I have fed this to friends, family and guests from afar, and all have thoroughly enjoyed it without any awareness that it was made with a meat substitute.

Recipe makes approximately 4-6 servings depending on portion size.

INGREDIENTS

1½lb (680g) potatoes, peeled and washed
1 bag (300g) Quorn mince
1 large onion, chopped
2 cloves garlic, crushed
2 tablespoons olive oil
1 heaped teaspoon Marmite
1 vegetable stock cube
14oz (400g) tin chopped tomatoes
2 tablespoons tomato puree
1 small glass of red or white wine

1 level teaspoon ground cinnamon
ground sea salt and freshly ground black pepper

CHEESE SAUCE

2oz (56g) butter
2oz (56g) plain flour
1 pint (568mls) milk, warmed
4oz (113g) strong cheddar cheese, grated
2oz (56g) strong cheddar cheese, grated for the topping

METHOD

1. Place the potatoes in boiling water, and cook for about 15 minutes, then drain.
2. Allow to cool a little, then cut into rings about 1cm thick.
3. In a saucepan, fry the onion and garlic in the olive oil until soft. Add the Quorn mince, stirring to break up the lumps as it defrosts.
4. Add the tinned tomatoes, tomato puree, wine, cinnamon, vegetable stock cube and 1 heaped teaspoon Marmite. Season to taste with salt and pepper.
5. Bring to the boil, reduce heat and simmer gently for 5 minutes, stirring regularly.

METHOD FOR CHEESE SAUCE

6. Melt the butter in a non stick pan.
7. Remove from the heat and add the flour, stirring well with a wooden spoon until a thick paste is formed. Return to a low heat for a couple of minutes, stirring continuously. Remove from the heat.
8. Gradually add the milk and blend in stirring well. I find this works much better if the milk is heated first as it speeds up the thickening process and the sauce is less likely to stick or burn.
9. Bring the sauce to simmering point, stirring continuously to prevent lumps forming for a

couple of minutes until it has thickened.

10. Stir 4oz (113g) grated cheese into the sauce over a low heat until the cheese has melted.

11. In a 3 pint oven proof dish, put a layer of the Quorn mixture, then a layer of potato slices. Repeat these layers until all the mixture and potatoes have been used up.

12. Pour the cheese sauce evenly over the top. Sprinkle remaining 2oz (56g) cheese over the top and bake in the centre of the oven for 30-40 minutes at 180°C (350°F) or Gas mark 4, until the top is golden brown.

Serve with a green salad and freshly baked bread.

Tagine

This is my version of this fantastic Moroccan dish. It is traditionally made with lamb, and is full of flavours that are somehow unique to anything you have ever tasted before. It is a dish that is sweet, fruity, and yet spicy. It conjurers up the very essence of its North African origins.

Recipe will make approximately 4-6 servings depending on portion size.

INGREDIENTS

1 medium to large onion, chopped
1 small red chilli, finely chopped
1 tablespoon olive oil
1 bag (300g) Quorn pieces
pinch each of dried rosemary, thyme and basil
12 fluid oz (340mls) stock made with 1 vegetable stock cube
3oz (85g) dates, chopped

3oz (85g) apricots, chopped
½ teaspoon cumin
½ teaspoon ginger
½ teaspoon cinnamon
5 fluid oz (142mls) pomegranate juice
1 dessert spoon cornflour
rice or couscous to serve

N.B. Use Quorn vegan pieces to turn this recipe into a great vegan alternative.

METHOD

1. Heat the olive oil in a large non stick pan and gently cook the onion and chilli until soft. Add the Quorn pieces and cook for a few minutes, stirring well.

2. Add the stock, dried herbs, dates, apricots, cumin, ginger, and cinnamon. Bring to the boil, stirring regularly, then add the pomegranate juice.

3. Simmer for about 10-15 minutes until the Quorn and dried fruit are cooked through.

4. Mix the cornflour with enough cold water to make a runny paste and pour into the Tagine, stirring continually as the sauce thickens to prevent lumps forming. Simmer for a few more minutes to ensure the cornflour has thickened the mixture sufficiently. Add a little extra water if the consistency becomes too thick.

'N.B. I have used a carton of Pomegranate juice for this recipe. Freshly squeezed Pomegranate juice could be used instead, but the recipe would lose some of its sweetness, which some people may prefer.

Serve with either plain boiled rice or couscous.

Thank You

This my chance to give a huge thank you to to all the people who helped to make this book happen.

I would like to thank Marlow Foods for their support in the early stages of this book, for believing in me and allowing me to use the brand name 'Quorn' in my recipes.

I would also like to thank Unilever for reviewing my recipes and allowing me to use the brand name 'Marmite' in my book.

This book would not have been possible without the continued support of my husband in all areas, from spending many hours listening to me and playing with the original layout of the book, to cropping and archiving photographs, reviewing and modifying the original text documents, tasting the meals, and not least of all thinking of the title.

Thank you also to my 3 wonderful girls who were the guinea pigs for some of my recipes, along with friends and family.

This book would have been far less professional had it not been for my friend Erica, who has not only painstakingly read and corrected every version, but has also encouraged me, and made me believe I could actually do this.

Thank you to my daughter Molly for her excellent photographs on the front cover and thumb nail pictures at the start of each section.

Thank you to Mairi McKenzie Photography and Charlie Dean Photography for their work on the back cover. Thanks also to Mairi for her photographs in the introductory and thank you pages.

Thank you to Clive Fisher for his superb image editing assistance.

Thank you James Irving [Uncle Jimmy] for being a catalyst for my original idea and providing inspiration for the title.

Thank you also to my designer and publisher for all their patience and support.

Kind regards,
Sarah

Some Interesting Reading!

Avoiding meat and dairy is the 'single biggest way' to reduce your impact on Earth.

> Damian Carrington. Environment editor. The Guardian.Thursday 31st May 2018.

Why eating less meat is the best thing you can do for the planet in 2019.

> Oliver Milman. The Guardian. Friday 21st December 2018.

Less is More. Reducing meat and dairy for a healthier life and planet.

> Greenpeace. March 2018.

The Paris Climate Agreement.

> 12th December 2015.

Antibiotic use in farm animals 'threatens human health'.

> NHS. 9th December 2015.

Nutrition and the risk of Alzheimer's disease.

> BioMed Research International Volume 2013. Article ID 524820. 10th June 2013.

Eating more red meat over time is associated with an increased risk of type 2 diabetes. A follow up of three studies of about 149,000 men and women.

> Jama Internal Medicine. A Jama Network publication. 17th June 2013.

A striking link has been revealed linking red meat consumption and the risk of developing cancer and heart disease.

> Viva Health. 12th March 2012.

70% of food poisoning is caused by contaminated animal flesh.

> The U.S. Department of Agriculture (USDA) 25th June 2010.

Vegetarian Food for Carnivores

Recipe Index

"Man makes use of flesh not out of want and necessity, seeing he has the liberty to make his choice of herbs and fruits, the plenty of which is inexhaustible - but out of luxury purchased by the slaughter of living beings. He shows himself more cruel than the most savage of wild beasts."

Plutarch AD 46 - 120

BV - #0049 - 170821 - C162 - 250/190/11 [13] - CB - 9781912419845 - Matt Lamination